Landmarks of world literature

Virginia Woolf

Landmarks of world literature

General Editor: J. P. Stern

Dickens: *Bleak House* – Graham Storey
Homer: *The Iliad* – Michael Silk
Dante: *The Divine Comedy* – Robin Kirkpatrick
Rousseau: *Confessions* – Peter France
Goethe: *Faust. Part One* – Nicholas Boyle
Woolf: *The Waves* – Eric Warner

FORTHCOMING
Cervantes: *Don Quixote* – Manuel Duran
Goethe: *The Sorrows of Young Werther* – Martin Swales
Constant: *Adolphe* – Dennis Wood
Balzac: *Old Goriot* – David Bellos
Mann: *Buddenbrooks* – Hugh Ridley
Pasternak: *Dr Zhivago* – Angela Livingstone
Marquez: *100 Years of Solitude* – Michael Wood

VIRGINIA WOOLF

The Waves

ERIC WARNER

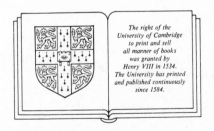

The right of the
University of Cambridge
to print and sell
all manner of books
was granted by
Henry VIII in 1534.
The University has printed
and published continuously
since 1584.

CAMBRIDGE UNIVERSITY PRESS

Cambridge
London   New York   New Rochelle
Melbourne   Sydney

Published by the Press Syndicate of the University of Cambridge
The Pitt Building, Trumpington Street, Cambridge CB2 1RP
32 East 57th Street, New York, NY 10022, USA
10 Stamford Road, Oakleigh, Melbourne 3166, Australia

First published 1987

Printed in Great Britain at
the University Press, Cambridge

British Library cataloguing in publication data
Warner, Eric
Virginia Woolf: The waves. –
(Landmarks of world literature)
1. Woolf, Virginia. Waves, The
I. Title   II. Series
823'.912   PR6045.072W3

Library of Congress cataloguing in publication data
Warner, Eric, 1951–
Virginia Woolf, the waves.
(Landmarks of world literature)
Bibliography.
1. Woolf, Virginia, 1882–1941. Waves.
I. Title.   II. Series.
PR6045.072W3388   1986   823'.912   86–9615

ISBN 0 521 32820 9 hard covers
ISBN 0 521 31563 8 paperback

GG

Contents

Chronology

	Virginia Woolf's life and work	Literary and cultural events	Historical developments
1882	Adeline Virginia Stephen born, third of four children to Leslie Stephen and Julia Duckworth; father appointed editor *Dictionary of National Biography*	D. G. Rossetti dies; Anthony Trollope dies; James Joyce born	Phoenix Park murders in Dublin
1885		Ezra Pound born; George Meredith – *Diana of the Crossways*; Walter Pater – *Marius the Epicurean*; John Ruskin – *Praeterita*	Salisbury becomes Prime Minister; Fall of Khartoum
1890	Virginia begins writing and editing family newspaper, *Hyde Park Gate News*	William Morris – *News From Nowhere*; James Frazer begins publishing *The Golden Bough*; Wm James – *The Principles of Psychology*	
1895	Death of mother; Virginia's first mental breakdown	Joseph Conrad – *Almayer's Folly*; Thomas Hardy – *Jude the Obscure*; Oscar Wilde – *The Importance of Being Earnest*; H. G. Wells – *The Time Machine*	Huxley dies; National Trust formed; Röntgen discovers x-rays; Freud's first work on psychoanalysis; Marconi's 'wireless' telegraphy perfected

1899	Thoby Stephen enters Trinity College, Cambridge; meets nucleus of future 'Bloomsbury Group' – Lytton Strachey, Leonard Woolf, Clive Bell	Henry James – *The Awkward Age*; George Gissing – *The Crown of Life*; Arthur Symons – *The Symbolist Movement in Literature*; Edward Elgar – *Enigma Variations*	Boer War begins
1900		Ruskin dies; Wilde dies; Conrad – *Lord Jim*	Relief of Ladysmith and Mafeking; Boxer Rebellion; First Zeppelin flight; Max Planck's Quantum Theory; Central London Railway (Tube) opens
1902	Leslie Stephen knighted	Henry James – *The Wings of the Dove*; Arnold Bennett – *Anna of the Five Towns*; Conrad – *The Heart of Darkness*	End of Boer War; Balfour becomes Prime Minister
1904	Death of Sir Leslie Stephen from cancer; Virginia's second mental breakdown; move to 46 Gordon Square, Bloomsbury with sister Vanessa and brother Adrian; publication of first review (unsigned) in *The Manchester Guardian*	Christopher Isherwood born; Conrad – *Nostromo*; Henry James – *The Golden Bowl*; Hardy – *The Dynasts*	Russo–Japanese War; *Entente Cordiale* between Britain and France
1905	Stephen children's trip to Greece	E. M. Forster – *Where Angels Fear to Tread*; Wilde – *De Profundis*; Wells – *Kipps*	Einstein's *Theory of Relativity*; Suffragettes active; motor omnibuses introduced in London

1906	Thoby Stephen dies of typhoid	Samuel Beckett born; Edward FitzGerald – *The Rubiyat of Omar Khayyam*; John Galsworthy – *A Man of Property*	Liberal government, Campbell-Bannerman becomes Prime Minister; Bakerloo and Piccadilly tube lines opened
1907	Vanessa Stephen marries Clive Bell; Virginia begins work on *Melymbrosia*, to become her first novel	W. H. Auden born; Louis MacNeice born; Conrad – *The Secret Agent*; Forster – *The Longest Journey*; J. M. Synge – *The Playboy of Western World*; A. R. Orage's *New Age* begins publication; George Bernard Shaw – *Major Barbara*	
1909	Seven chapters of draft novel, *Melymbrosia*, read and criticized by Clive Bell	Pound – *Personae*; Wells – *Tono-Bungay*, *Ann Veronica*	Bleriot flies the Channel
1910	Virginia meets Roger Fry; first Post-Impressionist Exhibition, organized by Fry, opens at Grafton Galleries in London	William Holman Hunt dies; Forster – *Howard's End*; Bennett – *Clayhanger*; W.B.Yeats – *The Green Helmet*; Bertrand Russell and Alfred North Whitehead – *Principia Mathematica*; Igor Stravinsky – *The Fire-Bird*	Edward VII dies; accession of George V
1912	Virginia marries Leonard Woolf; Leonard assists Fry with Second Post-Impressionist Exhibition in London	Pound – *Ripostes*; Roger Fry organizes second Post-Impressionist Exhibition	Home Rule Bill; Marconi Affair; Titanic sunk

Year			
1913	Completes first novel, *Voyage Out*; third mental breakdown	Robert Bridges becomes Poet Laureate; Conrad – *Chance*; Marcel Proust – *Swann's Way*; D. H. Lawrence – *Sons and Lovers*; Stravinsky – *Rite of Spring*; *The New Statesman* founded	Completion of Panama Canal
1914	Convalescing all year	Wyndham Lewis and Pound begin editing *Blast*; Joyce – *The Dubliners*; Shaw – *Androcles and the Lion*	First World War begins
1915	*The Voyage Out* published; Virginia begins keeping regular diary	Lawrence – *The Rainbow*; Ford Madox Ford – *The Good Soldier*; Conrad – *Victory*	Asquith becomes Prime Minister in coalition government
1916		Henry James dies; Joyce – *Portrait of the Artist*; Shaw – *Pygmalion*	Lloyd George Prime Minister; battles of Somme and Verdun; Easter Rising in Dublin
1917	Virginia contributing regularly to *TLS*; Woolfs initiate *Hogarth Press* with publication of *Two Stories*, including 'The Mark on the Wall'	Eliot – *Prufrock and Other Observations*; Pound – *Homage to Sextius Propertius*	Russian Revolution; U.S. enters war against Germany
1918	Reads part of manuscript of *Ulysses* for possible publication by Hogarth Press	Lytton Strachey – *Eminent Victorians*; Gerard Manley Hopkins – *Poems* (ed. Bridges); Joyce – *Exiles*	Armistice 11 November; end of First World War

Year		
1919	Publication of second novel *Night and Day*; 'Modern Fiction'	Eliot – *Poems* (Hogarth Press)	Treaty of Versailles; Amritsar Massacre in India; Rutherford splits the atom
1920	Completes more short stories – including 'Kew Gardens' and 'An Unwritten Novel'	Eliot – *The Sacred Wood*; Pound – *Hugh Selwyn Mauberley*; Lawrence – *Women in Love*; Yeats – *Michael Robartes and the Dancer*	League of Nations formed
1922	Third novel, *Jacob's Room*, published by Hogarth Press; first meeting with Vita Sackville-West	Proust dies; Eliot – *The Waste Land*; Joyce – *Ulysses* (in Paris); Galsworthy – *The Forsyte Saga*	Bonar Law becomes Prime Minister; Fascist Revolution in Italy
1924	Lectures in Cambridge on contemporary fiction; 'Mr Bennett and Mrs Brown' published by Hogarth Press later in the year	Conrad dies; Franz Kafka dies; Forster – *A Passage to India*; Ford – *Some Do Not* (beginning of tetrology *Parade's End*); T. E. Hulme – *Speculations*	Lenin dies; Ramsay Macdonald becomes Prime Minister in Labour Government, succeeded by Baldwin and Conservatives later in year
1925	Publication of fourth novel, *Mrs Dalloway*; publication of first collection of essays, *The Common Reader*	Ford – *No More Parades*; Yeats – *A Vision*; Aldous Huxley – *Those Barren Leaves*	
1926	30 September – diary entry recording vision of 'fin passing far out', origin of *The Waves*	Forster – *Aspects of the Novel*; Robert Graves and Laura Riding publish *A Survey of Modernist Poetry*	General Strike; Schrödinger's wave equation formulated – basis of quantum mechanics

1926	23 November – First diary entry of idea for 'semi-mystic profound life of a woman', which was to grow into *The Waves*	
1927	5 May – *To the Lighthouse* published	Lindberg flies the Atlantic
	18 May – Lectures at Oxford on 'Poetry, Fiction and the Future'	
1928	11 October – *Orlando*, a fantasy-biography published, dedicated to Vita Sackville-West	Hardy dies; Lawrence – *Lady Chatterley's Lover*; Huxley – *Point Counter Point*
	20 October – Woolf reads two papers to women's colleges, subsequently to become *A Room of One's Own*	
1929	*A Room of One's Own* published	Yeats – *The Winding Stair*; C. Day Lewis – *Transitional Poems*; MacNeice – *Blind Fireworks*; Graves – *Goodbye to All That*
		Labour Government, Macdonald becomes Prime Minister; Collapse of New York Stock Exchange leading to world recession

1930	April – Completes first version of *The Waves*, known as *The Moths*; June – starts on second version; August – 'Resolving into series of dramatic soliloquies'	Lawrence dies; Auden – *Poems*; Eliot – *Ash Wednesday*; Harold Pinter born	
1931	7 February – completes second version of *The Waves* 8 October – *The Waves* published	Arnold Bennett dies	
1932	Publication of *Common Reader, Second Series*; death of Lytton Strachey	Auden – *The Orators*; Huxley – *Brave New World*	Roosevelt elected President, U.S.A.
1936	Completes *The Years*, after much struggle and torment	Rudyard Kipling dies; Eliot – *Collected Poems 1909–35*; Auden – *Look Stranger*; Yeats – *Oxford Book of Modern Verse*	Civil War in Spain; George V dies; accession and abdication of Edward VIII; accession of George VI
1937	Publication of *The Years*, her eighth novel; Julian Bell killed in Spanish Civil War, driving ambulance for the Republicans	David Jones – *In Parenthesis*; George Orwell – *Road to Wigan Pier*	Chamberlain Prime Minister; destruction of Guernica
1938	*Three Guineas*, feminist pamphlet, published; Begins work on *Poyntz Hall* (to become final novel, *Between the Acts*)	Beckett – *Murphy*; Graham Greene – *Brighton Rock*; Orwell – *Homage to Catalonia*	Munich Agreement

1939	April – begins writing important autobiographical memoir, 'A Sketch of the Past'	Yeats dies; Ford dies; MacNeice – *Autumn Journal*; Joyce – *Finnegans Wake*; Isherwood – *Goodbye to Berlin*; Henry Green – *Party Going*; Orwell – *Coming up for Air*	Spanish Civil War ends; pact between Hitler and Stalin; Germany invades Poland; start of Second World War
1940	Completes biography of *Roger Fry*	Yeats – *Last Poems*; Auden – *Another Time*; Arthur Koestler – *Darkness at Noon*; Orwell – *Inside the Whale and Other Essays*	Churchill Prime Minister; Nazi occupation of France; evacuation from Dunkirk; Battle of Britain
1941	Completes *Between the Acts* in February; commits suicide by drowning, 28 March	Joyce dies; Auden – *New Year Letter*	German invasion of Russia; Japanese attack on Pearl Harbor

Preface

The Waves is Virginia Woolf's most formidable and challenging work of art. She herself regarded it as 'the most difficult and complex' of her books, and few readers since its publication in 1931 have dissented from this judgement. In this, her seventh major work of fiction, she took that passion for experiment which created the great novels of her middle career to its 'furthest development so far', and the result is unique, both within her own *oeuvre* and the larger tradition of English fiction itself. Her most formally inventive fiction, *The Waves* appears to owe its inspiration more to poetry and drama than the novel, as six speakers engage in a ceaseless round of monologues or 'soliloquies' about the course and development of their lives. Here Woolf freely manipulated conventional elements of fiction − plot, character, narrative − in a concerted attempt to take the novel beyond its customary compass. The results have been predictable, and shared by many modernist works of art: intense admiration by a few is balanced against extreme bafflement on the part of the common reader. Many have felt that the work in some sense goes too far, evolving beyond the bounds of what one can recognizably call a novel. Yet one of the many paradoxes of *The Waves* is that its difficulties are deceptive, to some extent superficial; once past the initial challenge of the form one finds many links with the rest of Woolf's art, as indeed with the novel itself. It is the aim of this volume to help the reader look beneath the dazzling surface of *The Waves*, to remove some of the obstacles which have blocked the way to a clearer perception of this strange, inspired and unforgettable work which has steadily won a place among the handful of great imaginings of the twentieth century.

Chapter 1

Introduction

Initial bearings

An analysis of *The Waves* must begin with an acknowledge-
ment of the difficulties that stand in the way of our initial
approach to the work, difficulties of a rather peculiar kind.
A comparison with James Joyce, an author with whom Virginia
Woolf is often linked, may be helpful here. In its formal
experimentation, its implied attack on conventional aspects of
the novel, *The Waves* is analogous to *Finnegans Wake* —
though there is no evidence that she read the 'Work in
Progress', as it was called at the time, or that the acute
consciousness of Joyce which stimulated her earlier efforts
extended to this work. The comparison is revealing, however.
Like the *Wake*, *The Waves* deliberately strives for the palm
of innovation so assiduously courted by modernist art; and,
like it, Woolf's book has inspired a debate about whether or
not it can be called a novel. There is the further similarity in
that, while agreeing that *The Waves* represents her highest
aesthetic endeavour, few readers are willing to claim it as her
most satisfying effort; there remains something unsettling in
the dazzling display of technique, something which, as in the
case of Joyce's final work, renders the book overly enigmatic
and elusive. Both fictions might thus be said to illustrate
another great modernist desire, in the words of Wallace Stevens
to 'resist the intelligence, almost successfully' — and in both
cases that success has been too close for comfort. Considered
opinion continues to plump for *Ulysses* as Joyce's masterpiece,
just as Virginia Woolf's common reader prefers her earlier,
more accessible novels, *Mrs Dalloway* and *To the Lighthouse*.

Even so, both works have had their champions. Leonard
Woolf, in some respects his wife's ideal reader, instantly
pronounced *The Waves* 'a masterpiece', a view from which he

never wavered. Another acute reader, Stuart Hampshire, expressed a similar preference, likening the book to 'a great Fauve painting' where the impact of the whole was so great as to override an inability clearly to mark or discriminate its parts. Given the current critical taste for indeterminacy, and for works which appear to refute or undermine their comprehensible meaning by creating an enclosed, entirely self-referential realm, one might expect that the prestiege of both works would continue to rise in tandem. But as yet *The Waves* has not followed the *Wake*'s elevation to the pantheon of 'post-modern' texts. Indeed this is where the comparison to *Finnegans Wake* begins to break down, and ultimately the contrasts between the two works become more striking and informative than their similarities. For Woolf's work has nothing of the verbal opacity of Joyce's; that intense distortion of the medium itself, the rending of words which the Irishman pursues with such extravagance and power, has no part in Virginia Woolf's book. For this reason the difficulties of approaching the *Wake*, its hard, repellent, self-enclosed quality at first reading, are not an issue in *The Waves*. Precisely the reverse is true; paradoxically, for all its radical explorations Woolf's book often seems if anything too clear, too transparent and inviting. Most critics who have written on *The Waves* have remarked on just this seductive quality, the way in which the beckoning and pellucid prose of the book seems to absorb one, dissolve readers in its own verbal fluidity. Unlike the opaque bafflements of Joyce's multiverse, Woolf's sea of words is one in which the critical faculty, if not drowned, is at least swept away. Elizabeth Hardwick, for example, has given memorable expression to this feeling:

I was immensely moved by *The Waves* when I read it recently and yet I cannot think of anything to say except that it was wonderful. The people are not characters, there is no plot in the usual sense. What can you bring to bear: verisimilitude to what? You can merely say over and over again, very beautiful, and that when you were reading it you were happy.

Glossing this comment, Ian Gregor has remarked that '*The Waves* has choreographed the reader's meditations and left no margin for critical discourse', a view which echoes Stuart

Hampshire's comment that 'the reader of *The Waves* is left helpless, either overwhelmed or repelled, . . . without the independent material on which his imagination can work. The implications are already stated, the novel criticizes itself.' Such comments suggest the difficulty which criticism has had with this work. For one of the greatest peculiarities of *The Waves* is that it seems to be all on the surface; the six figures whose speech absorbs the narrative are in a sense critics themselves, perpetually engaged in an attempt to read the text of their lives, and establish the patterns, links, recurrent motifs, structures contained therein. The flow of language which issues from them is one of remorseless analysis, as they constantly, overtly attempt to assess the pattern and significance of their lives, to gauge the distance between surface and symbol. Herein lies the principal contrast with *Finnegans Wake*: through the dislocated language Joyce attempts to plumb the subconscious depths of the mind, exploring the 'night world' of half-articulated speech. *The Waves*, however, is among the most self-conscious works ever written, a continual dramatized process of self-awareness; and this does appear to leave little room for critical endeavour. For those willing to submit to such currents the work has its pleasures, as Hardwick attests; but the effect is not universally agreeable. So acute a reader as Frank Kermode has confessed to feeling 'sick' while immersed in *The Waves*, and this unsettling is not atypical.

Paradoxically, then, the work's difficulties have put readers off while its very openness and immediacy has made it resistant to criticism. This suggests that the first step to approaching *The Waves* is to draw back, gaining some distance and perspective, from which a more judicious assessment may be made. Let us begin our attempt to examine the book by situating it within the broader context of Virginia Woolf's career, her life and times.

A modern outlook

As the preceding chronology suggests, Virginia Woolf lived through interesting times. Simplifying greatly, this can be described as a time of transition, encompassing the movement from the latter part of the high Victorian era to the new forms and energies of the twentieth century. There is no doubt that the experience of this transformation had a profound effect on Woolf; it appears in some form in all her novels, most clearly in works such as *To the Lighthouse* and *The Years*, where the change in the lives of the characters explicitly parallels the larger historical movement from Victorian to modern times. But there are deeper effects. It is the nature of such transitions to involve an uneasy meeting of old and new, past and present, and to engender conflicts or tensions out of their meeting. Such a duality shows up in broad terms in Woolf's steady devotion to the institution of marriage within the increasingly 'liberated' ambiance of Bloomsbury, or her refusal to be psychoanalysed even though her brother was one of Freud's pupils and her press published the English translations of his works. More subtly, there was a marked conflict within her imagination itself: 'Now is life very solid, or very shifting? I am haunted by the two contradictions' (4 Jan. 1929). This diary entry was written while she was engaged in composing *The Waves*, but the duality suggested here is in fact a central element of Woolf's imaginative life. Her fiction is pervaded by the opposition between order and freedom, security and promise, value and discovery, stability and movement, and no work is more imbued with this conflict than *The Waves*. To a great extent this grows out of the circumstances of her own life, and the particular context in which the book was written; as a prelude to examining the work in detail it is thus necessary to explore this context further.

In effect, Woolf's life, like that of her exact contemporary Joyce, spans the birth of the modern age. This is relevant because her contribution to that birth is one of the reasons for which she is remembered and valued today. She is renowned as one of the architects of the modern novel, flourishing amid the great modernist revolution in the arts in the early decades of the present century. We scarcely have space to enter fully into the great debate as to 'what was modernism', even if the undertaking were profitable. For the sake of convenience let us agree (as most wise critics have done) to limit the era of high modernism to the first three decades of the twentieth century. Within that span one can identify a series of shared assumptions, a broad sense of common purpose, which may loosely define a movement in the arts. The main features of this movement have often been sketched. The writers and artists who participated in it were largely urban, cosmopolitan intellectuals. One consequence of this was the prominence given to the city in their works, as the modern, urban backdrop to *The Wasteland*, *Ulysses*, and *Mrs Dalloway* testifies. Another was a polyglot openness to foreign influences, which helped to engender an international aspect to the movement. This is readily seen in the widespread influence which Le Corbusier and the Bauhaus exercised on European furniture and design; but more local and specifically literary examples are not hard to find – the impact of Laforgue on Eliot, of Ibsen on Joyce, of Proust on Virginia Woolf is well known. The import in every case was to help to escape from what was deemed native insularity, and, among other thing, such foreign colour helped to make the work of the modernist dense, allusive and opaque to the common reader, a fact which suited the temper of the times very well. For the great modernists were heirs to the Aesthetic Movement of the previous century, rejecting the mass audience and its progressive commercialization of art, just as they repudiated the petty bourgeoisie of the commercial middle classes who were its consumers. By and large they wrote for a small enclave of intelligentsia, and had no qualms about making their work difficult and obscure. Esoteric allusions abounded, along with a persistent trend toward compression, contraction, condensation, suspending the ordered, sequential logic, the easy-to-follow train of thought which had triumphed in the discursive moralizing of the previous century. The kind of pandering to the values of the audience which had engaged such Victorian writers as Dickens, Trollope and Tennyson was regarded as anathema; discursiveness was rejected in favour of economy, density and concentration. To 'make it new' in Pound's vital phrase was to make it complex, multi-faceted, opaque, ordered by an aesthetic logic far removed from common or conventional comprehension.

Contrary to the impression given by some of the polemics and propaganda of the 'revolution', however, the mainspring in the condensed art of modernism was not an attack on the audience. Rather it was the sense of having entered a new age, one in which the pressure of experience became substantially greater, and more bewildering, than ever before. It has often been observed that such intellectual tumult had been going on throughout the nineteenth century, which is true enough; and just as often that the change in the twentieth century was one of degree which amounted to one of kind. Such eminent Victorians as Matthew Arnold, George Eliot, even Woolf's father, Leslie Stephen, exemplify the nineteenth-century tendency to lay aside central tenets of belief while retaining the standards, values, assumptions, and forms of conduct pertaining to those beliefs. The moderns, however, were not granted such repose; the intelligent mind of the early twentieth century had to contend with Einstein's Theory of Relativity, Freud's investigations into the irrational nature of the human psyche, technical and technological advances of every kind − all accumulating to produce the accelerating explosion of cultural energy foreseen in Henry Adams's autobiography at the turn of the century. All this was destructive of coherence, even the displaced or marginal coherence which sustained the Victorians. The modern world view was 'apocalyptic', feeling the destructive element too fully. It was now an age of shoring fragments against ruins, an age whose complexity could not be contained in accepted styles, and which thus appeared to demand a new art, with forms and strategies appropriate to its bewildering, multiplex character.

All of this led to a sense of 'movement', conscious of itself and, more important, consciously revolutionary. It was a time of manifestoes, of proclamations, of little magazines heralding the 'new age' to small circulations. 'In or about December, 1910', wrote Virginia Woolf, 'human character changed.' The dominant sense of the age was of the changed circumstances, changes which were embraced as the necessary condition of genuinely new art. This gave the era a significant revolutionary flavour, which was most immediately and tellingly revealed in technique or form, where conventions are most keenly felt and changes most visible. It is not surprising, therefore, that formal experiment became the hallmark of modernist art. The date Woolf chose to mark the change was that of the first Post-Impressionist Exhibition, which exposed the bizarre new forms of contemporary European painters to an unbelieving Edwardian audience in London, and revealed in a powerful visual expression the new conceptions of reality abroad. It was not long before equivalent formal dislocations spread to other media, and in one's encounter with contemporary literary works of the period — the fragmented images of Eliot, or Joyce's splintered mosaic — it is the aggressive formalization that is most immediately striking.

It was to this era of bold new energies and restless formal experiment that Virginia Woolf belonged. She was acutely aware of the main aesthetic thrust of her age, not only from her association with Fry and the modern painters. The company she keeps in her diaries — Henry James, T. S. Eliot, James Joyce, Marcel Proust — show her to have been well aware of the major literary talents of the age, measuring her own work and efforts against theirs. Indeed it is precisely *as* a novelist that Woolf's awareness of the age was sharpened, for the revolutionary changes in form and feeling were brought into focus by prose fiction in a distinctive way. In the hands of the great nineteenth-century masters the novel had risen to the dominant and most popular form of literary art, and as such had come to be seen as a unique repository of social values. The work of Jane Austen, Scott, Thackeray, Dickens, George Eliot, and Trollope, however critical or reformist its message, had suggested that human life was social life, and that the parameters of that society formed a large and stable cultural tradition. It was just this cultural stability which was called into question by developments in the early twentieth century. The novel reflected the full force of this change, and for many the massively erudite experiments of Joyce, with their fragmented and subjective portrayal of experience, seemed the most telling expression of the age. Similarly, precursors of this experimental ethos, such as Flaubert and Proust, Conrad and Henry James, were revered by the high modernist figures of Eliot and Pound. Paradoxically, the novel retained its mimetic preserve of reflecting 'life', but the image of life reflected was now changeable and unsettling, eccentric and unique. 'Modern' fiction was difficult, disturbing and disruptive, seeming to crystallize the radical tenor of the age.

Virginia Woolf, whose press first published *The Waste Land* and considered bringing out *Ulysses*, was fully exposed to these developments; and as a novelist herself was not slow to kindle an answering enthusiasm. As she entered her artistic maturity, she quickly became an outspoken proponent of a modernist outlook, publishing a series of polemical essays which urged the necessity for English fiction to cast off the constraints and conventions of the past, and which vigorously attacked the popular Edwardian novelists of the day as being out of step with the times. For the modern temper, she wrote, 'the accent falls differently from of old', the point of interest lies elsewhere than 'is commonly thought', within, as she put it, 'the dark places of psychology'. In irritation she asked: must novels go on being descriptive, externalized, implying a stable point of view and widely shared assumptions about the nature of reality? Is life like this?

Look within and life, it seems, is very far from being like this. Examine for a moment an ordinary mind on an ordinary day. The mind receives a myriad impressions – trivial, fantastic, evanescent, or engraved with the sharpness of steel. From all sides they come, an incessant shower of innumerable atoms; and as they fall, as they shape themselves into the life of Monday or Tuesday, the accent falls differently from of old . . . Life is not a series of gig-lamps symmetrically arranged; life is a luminous halo, a semi-transparent envelope surrounding us from the beginning of consciousness to the end . . .

Let us record the atoms as they fall upon the mind in the order in which they fall, let us trace the pattern, however disconnected and incoherent in appearance, which each sight or incident scores upon the consciousness.

The 'disconnected pattern' might serve as an epigraph to the modern age itself, and this passage has long been seen as Woolf's modernist manifesto. The emphasis here, in her essay 'Modern Fiction' (1919), is clearly on a shift from outer to inner reality, from action and event to perception and response, from 'what was previously thought large' to what was thought small. And there is ample evidence that Woolf in her fiction pursued the course she outlined here. In her diary entries throughout the 1920s, for example, we find her sketching out ideas for some 'new form for a new kind of novel', a work of prose fiction which would be 'crepuscular', 'no scaffolding to be seen' – removing, that is, the heavy props of contrived plot, narratorial machinations and externally defined characters. Her greatest works, moreover, are imbued with a corresponding sense of exciting formal experiment and discovery; progressively we find her throwing off the prosaic discursiveness, the homage to agreed values and external descriptions which had supported much of Victorian fiction, in a concerted effort to bring the novel closer to the quick of the mind. Tired of old descriptions of the world, she sought to centre her art on the notion of individual reality, patterning her narrative movement on what William James called the 'stream-of-consciousness' – unstable, flickering, transient – as she traced the 'atoms' of sensation that fell on the mind. The point to make here, without exploring this aim in greater detail, is that in so doing she believed she was not only reflecting a more adequate representation of reality, but also participating in the spirit of the age, at one with the compeers whom she perceived to be in the process of creating a new order of art.

The sense of the past

It is true that any quick look at Woolf's career throws her modernism into prominence, and for a long time critics seized

upon her modern 'revolt' against the past as the most evident
and significant aspect of her art. Yet a closer look at her
chronology reveals contrary suggestions, chief among which
is the fact that her early and formative years were spent in the
nineteenth century. Indeed in many crucial respects she remains
deeply rooted in this period. To begin with, her father, Leslie
Stephen, was one of the foremost intellectuals of the late
Victorian age, editor of the distinguished journal, the *Cornhill
Magazine*, and subsequently principal overseer of one of the
great Victorian monuments, the *Dictionary of National
Biography*. His first wife was a daughter of Thackeray, and
the Stephen family itself was one of the most important
components of the famous 'Clapham Sect'. All this placed
Stephen at the summit of the Victorian intellectual aristocracy,
a fact which passed on to the young Virginia certain invaluable
gifts. She herself recalled being 'born into a very com-
municative, literate, letter writing, visiting, articulate, late
nineteenth century world', all attributes which marked her for
life. As a child she met most of the great writers, artists and
thinkers of the day, growing up in an atmosphere where books,
art, the life of the mind were an established and accepted part
of life. Moreover, her father's literary tastes and talents had
a profound effect on her own, and his example clearly inspired
her career as a writer. It was her father's library, for instance,
whereof he gave her free rein, in which she first discovered the
large and liberating possibilities of literature, and developed
a love of reading which lasted throughout her life. Perhaps
most significantly of all, however, Woolf's particular
upbringing provided a solid foundation in the high Liberal
world of the late nineteenth century, giving her a secure sense
of the worth of individual freedom and intellectual tolerance
which marked her critical and creative spirit for ever. (This is
the motive force behind her protest on behalf of women, for
example.) Though in time she came to reject the tastes and
temper of the older generation (as most independent children
do) the fact remains that all her life she was deeply attached
to and influenced by the liberal, tolerant, inquisitive spirit of
her father's world.

This would appear to be in stark contradiction with what we have observed of her modernist tendencies; but the contradiction must stand. Indeed a truer picture would be to say that Woolf retained a love-hate relation with modernism and the iconoclastic energies it released. It is this aspect of Virginia Woolf's character which explains her reverence for the 'great tradition' of English literature, the love with which she approached the novels of Defoe and Sterne, Jane Austen and George Eliot, Meredith and Hardy, which is so evident in her essays and diary. It likewise helps to account for her concern for the 'common reader' which breathes through her criticism, and for the acuteness, sensitivity and lucidity of her critical prose. Moreover, the attachment to her intellectual inheritance is also the reason why, though she welcomed the experiments of modernism, she found so much to complain of in its achievements. It is often forgotten that those same essays which boldly call for a new order of art, also qualify or deprecate the results of that trial so far − 'It is an age of fragments . . . incapable of sustained effort, and not to be compared with the age which went before', she claimed in 'How It Strikes a Contemporary' (1923); and in 'Modern Fiction', after giving high marks to the promising experiments of Mr Joyce, she notes with regret that *Ulysses* 'fails to compare' with such high examples of art as Conrad's *Youth* or Hardy's *The Mayor of Casterbridge*. In its haste to acclaim the 'modernist' Virginia Woolf, criticism has been too ready to overlook or ignore such statements. Of late there have been signs of a more balanced view emerging, which takes her devotion to the older order into account; but we need to keep in mind that there were other elements in her make-up than a singleminded attachment to the modernist cause.

Nowhere is this duality more clearly displayed than in that aspect of Woolf's life which has become of paramount interest in the present: Bloomsbury. The Bloomsbury Group has become so notorious in our day that, once again, it is hardly necessary to provide more than a background sketch. Briefly put, the Bloomsbury Group, or Circle, had its origins

in 1899, the year that Virginia's elder brother, Thoby
Stephen, went up to Cambridge. That same year Clive Bell,
Lytton Strachey and Leonard Woolf entered the university,
and it was around this nucleus that what became the
Bloomsbury Group was formed. The Group as such was fully
constituted only in 1904, when these graduates of Cambridge
moved to London, to a house in Gordon Square, Bloomsbury, and were joined by Thoby's two sisters, Vanessa and
Virginia. Thus began a relatively relaxed, bohemian life,
mixing work, pleasure and late-night conversation. The
Group expanded, incorporating J. M. Keynes, E. M. Forster
and Roger Fry, among others, and two of its members, Clive
Bell and Leonard Woolf, married the two Stephen sisters,
initiating a whole sequence of familial relations and
internecine squabbles, some of whose reverberations still
linger on today.

There is much that is both trivial and tedious in this Group,
which has been compounded by its over-exposure in the
numerous biographies, diaries and memoirs of every
conceivable satellite and hanger-on. Indeed the appellation of
'Group' is a misnomer, since there never was anything like a
concerted programme, or even an agreed aesthetic, as Lytton
Strachey's horrified reaction to the painters of the Group
reveals. What united the disparate collection of individuals
was personal friendship and a devotion to work, usually art
in the broadest possible sense. This helps to make sense of
the oft-quoted dictum that the Group's credo comes from
G. E. Moore's *Principia Ethica*, which states that the most
valuable things in life are certain states of consciousness
among which are the perception of beautiful objects and
personal relations.

What is important for our purposes is to recognize the
considerable effect which this Group had on Virginia Woolf.
She was to the end of her days vexed by the conjunction of
being extremely awkward and shy with strangers, yet having
an innately social disposition. It was thus a great boon to be
surrounded by a circle of intimates who were known, trusted
and supportive. This is particularly so with regard to her art;

she needed a steady supply of sympathy and encouragement in order to work productively, and by far the most important result of the Bloomsbury Group on Virginia Woolf was to promote and encourage her writing. She always lacked self-confidence and self-esteem, a fact which showed itself most forcefully at the completion of a novel, when she faced the traumatic prospect of seeing her work despatched to the world and made public. Her diaries are filled with expressions of waiting for her sister Vanessa's or E. M. Forster's or Lytton Strachey's reaction, almost as if the Group were a buffer from the world's view, and winning their approval would compensate for whatever fate the work enjoyed at large. In this sense it is clear that the sympathy and support of this close circle of intimates made it possible for her to go on writing.

On the face of it Woolf's central role in Bloomsbury would seem to mesh well with her devotion to modernism: both elements were engaged in a reaction to what was seen as outmoded, Victorian ways of feeling, thinking and acting, and both insisted on the right to make new valuations and judgements on the basis of personal experience. But the resemblance is superficial, and in fact the two currents flow in opposite directions. The fact is that Bloomsbury's revolt against their Victorian forebears was really a revolt in manners, a reaction to the 'forms of life' of their parents. The attack levelled by the Bloomsbury Group was on the gloomy seriousness, the stiff moral propriety of their predecessors, and the focus of the revolt is shown in the more relaxed behaviour and bohemian trappings of the Group − signified in the move from socially correct Kensington to *louche* Bloomsbury. Yet Bloomsbury was itself an avatar of the Victorian Liberal intellectual tradition (finely represented by Leslie Stephen), a tradition which yielded a high-minded, free-thinking gathering of the elect, intensely devoted to work and instilled with the rational belief in the values of civilization and order. Such a tradition produced an intellectual elite, confident in the powers of reason and supporting notions of order, harmony and civilized behaviour

– values which they believed were universally perceivable by sufficiently enlightened minds. (It is not suprising that so much of their thought paid homage to the eighteenth century, again a special interest of Leslie Stephen.) For all its cliquishness and sometimes irritating petulance and snobbery, Bloomsbury essentially advanced notions of civilized, liberated behaviour and personal judgement against the wildness and brutality (Forster's 'panic and emptiness') of the world ouside. In this they have more in common with J. S. Mill than with any of the great modernist figures of the twentieth century.

The moderns, on the other hand, reflected far more accurately the underlying dissolution and skepticism of the age. There is regret at the world which has been lost in *The Waste Land* or even *Ulysses*, but only through oblique reflection of its current fragments. There is, correspondingly, far less confidence in any notion of 'civilization' as an effective power. The values advanced by such modernist works, moreover, are those of an entirely individual, self-created ordering, a more solitary and anxious position advanced through the desperate strategies of their art. 'Things fall apart; the centre cannot hold' chanted Yeats, in what might be an epigraph for these artists, and lack of civilized order, the failure of widely shared cultural values is reflected in the fragmented, dislocated forms of their art. The notorious difficulty, the 'struggle of the modern', reflects this sense of having to make one's own way, of having lost the binding power of cultural norms and of having to create these through an imagined order alone. Ultimately, this extreme, solipsistic train runs directly counter to the Liberal, rational faith espoused by Bloomsbury.

The place of *The Waves*

A broad view of Woolf's life and times, then, reveals a play of contradictory forces, of cross-currents that grows out of the era of transition she inhabited. With this perspective in mind, we may begin to locate *The Waves* more precisely in its context, and explore how these conflicting elements affected the work.

We begin to situate *The Waves* by recognizing that the book was the final fruit of Virginia Woolf's great decade, 1920–30. This period was a watershed in Woolf's career, during which she experienced her greatest creative development and advance. Not coincidentally it was the period in which she was most aware of the modernist movement taking place around her. The Twenties saw her most important aesthetic manifestoes – the essays 'Modern Fiction' (1919), 'Mr Bennett and Mrs Brown' (1924), 'The Narrow Bridge of Art' (1927) – all calling for new directions and new focus for the novel. In each of these clarion calls, we can see her outlining the goal she was to pursue concurrently in her art, that of a more subjective and psychological reflection of life. In a remarkable sequence of works, following rapidly upon one another, she began to develop that 'new form for a new kind of novel' she longed to create. The sequence which stretched from *Jacob's Room* (1922) to *Mrs Dalloway* (1925) and *To the Lighthouse* (1927) progressively refined the technique of internalized narrative which focused the work 'within' the mind. As her confidence increased the writing grew more fluid, unchecked, sure, and she began, as she put it, 'to say something in my own voice', and in the process produced some of the classic works of modern fiction.

The Waves must first of all be seen as the culmination of this extraordinary period of inspiration, confidence and achievement. Published in 1931, this work rose out of the momentum generated by the preceding decade. The book was, as she wrote in her diary, 'my furthest development so far', the work in which she abandoned formal conventions most freely, thus reaching an experimental or innovative peak she had hardly conceived before. She called it 'my first work in my own style', and in retrospect the book certainly appears as some sort of summit, riding the crest of the wave of her modernist innovation. As indicated earlier, the severity of this experiment raises generic problems – indeed a highly paradoxical relation with 'the novel' is at the heart of the work. This subject involves complex and theoretical issues beyond the scope of our present purpose, and must be reserved for a later chapter. Here we are concerned with the context or place of *The Waves* within her career as a whole, and with hindsight the book appears to us as the culmination of her modernist period. This fact is thrown into relief by the striking change in direction which followed. Indeed as the Thirties were to change radically the tone and temper of the time, it is hardly going too far to see *The Waves* as one of the last fruits of modernism itself. Certainly for Woolf the following decade was a long trough, bringing the deaths of many close friends, the inexorable slide toward another world war, and, significantly for her, an age in which the formal aesthetic purism of the modernists was rejected in favour of a more committed, political art. Her subsequent novel, *The Years*, was an ill-fated attempt to adapt to these changes; but the work was ground out in a long, tortuous and painful struggle, not appearing until the decade was nearly over in 1937. The contrast with the quick, certain strides of the previous decade could not be greater. In the larger perspective, therefore, *The Waves* occupies a particularly interesting junction in Virginia Woolf's career, a work written at the height of her powers before a decline, and the climax of her 'modernist' phase.

With respect to what we might call Woolf's public or professional career, then, the period leading up to *The Waves* is one of increasing commitment to the fierce creative energies, the radical experiments of modernism. Yet the work flowed from personal or private sources as well, and these led in a different direction. *The Waves*, concentrating as it does on a close circle of intelligent, highly articulate friends, has often been seen as her tribute to Bloomsbury. There is truth in this, but it is important at this stage to set the influence in context. The fact is that Bloomsbury as an active, ongoing phenomenon lasted about a decade – during the period, roughly, from 1905 to 1915, when nearly all its members were living in close proximity to one another in London, and enjoying regular contact. This coincided, however, with the most crucial stage in Woolf's artistic career, the protracted period of composition of her first novel, *The Voyage Out*, drafts of which were given to Clive Bell for criticism. It was a period when she was most vulnerable and searching, and most in need of dependable surroundings, of sympathetic and supportive companions. Helping Woolf through this phase of her life was in a sense Bloomsbury's greatest service to her art, and she offered thanks in embodying most of the members of the Group at that time as characters in her first major work.

Yet after this period, from about the time of Woolf's marriage in 1912, the Bloomsbury Group progressively lost meaning. Its members dispersed through a series of moves, marriages and other liaisons; though for some time the links were maintained, the affection of 'old friends' kept up, gradually, the exciting sense of youth and discovery, the exploration of newer, freer life styles dissipated. In the period leading up to *The Waves* the sense of 'Old Bloomsbury' fell away almost completely: 'I seldom see Lytton now' she wrote in her diary; 'Bloomsbury being done with'. This was in part because during this period she was concentrating on her art, and the modernist experiments with which it was consumed. However, after the achievement of *To the Lighthouse* and a reassuring conviction that she had arrived artistically, Woolf increasingly turned to retrospect about the Group. Indeed absence of direct contact prompted her to reflect upon the Group in its early days, and to brood upon the meaning it had for her life. This brooding was connected with more general thoughts on ageing and death (never far from Woolf's mind), but also focused specifically on one event which had been of great significance to her as well as to Bloomsbury: the sudden death of her brother Thoby. Woolf always maintained that he had been destined for magnificence (a view that was shared), and that his senseless and fortuitous death was a tragedy. She had given some oblique expression to these feelings in *Jacob's Room* (1922), but the event resurfaced in her thoughts now, linked with its larger implications for the network of friendships and association that was Bloomsbury, and it crystallized in a decisive way in her book. The magnificent, silent figure of Percival in *The Waves* is based on Thoby, and in one sense the book is an elegy for him as *To the Lighthouse* had been an elegy for her parents. Indeed in the moment of relief and exaltation when she finished the final draft she wrote of her desire to inscribe his name and date on the title page (7 Feb. 1931). It is, however, possible to exaggerate this, since Percival serves primarily as a focus for the other six characters to move around, and it is the network of relations that is most apparent in the work. When, late in the book, one of the characters eulogizes over 'the dead body of all we have been and have not been', it is hard to mistake the implied elegy both to Thoby and his Bloomsbury companions.

Unity and division

The perspective gained by this quick look into the background suggests that a fruitful way of approaching *The Waves* is to regard it as the confluence of these two streams of influence: her professional, aesthetic allegiances to modernism married with her private, personal loyalties to Bloomsbury. But it was not a marriage of true minds, and the discordances account for much of the turbulence in the work. Given such contradictory influences we might expect there to be evidence of tension in the resulting work, and indeed this is not hard to find. The modernist influence is clearly visible, in the radical experiment with form she undertook in the work; but it is also evident in the anxious and solitary voices of the six speakers, the persistent failure of meaning or coherence which they face, and the remorseless pull toward separation and solitude which they endure (for all its saturated speech, there is no dialogue in the novel). This isolating movement is writ large in the book as a whole, which progresses from a succession of six speakers to one final soliloquy, significantly enough spoken by an artist figure trying to put the fragmented pieces of their lives together in one final ordering. The link with Eliot, Pound or Joyce is patent; yet such 'modernist' tendencies are countered by the strong communal drive in the work, the way in which the six individuals repeatedly form and re-form into a collective circle, and the way in which friendship sustains them against the forces of dissolution. Similarly, their incessant speech can also be read as a protest against incoherence, a momentary stay against confusion; their reflective and luminous talk clarifies experience in a way which works against fragmentation. The paradox of critical response to the work mentioned in the Preface here returns. For, in effect, the starkly experimental form which disrupts comprehension is undermined by the work's transparency, its persistent explanatory bent and concern to remove opacity. Thus the modernist aesthetic at work in the book is crossed by the urgency and immediacy with which it proclaims its message. For all its unusual form, we are most likely as readers to be aware of the book's ethical or humane dimension, of six human beings desperately seeking the answer to the question posed by Lily Briscoe in *To the Lighthouse*, 'What is the meaning of life?' – though, as we shall see, the assumption or hope that there is a meaning contends all the while with a more 'modern' scepticism which is mirrored in the dissolvent texture of the form.

Our survey of the background of *The Waves* thus provides us with a sense of the contrary or conflicting currents which went into the work and which marks the character of the whole. The book, seen in broad terms, reveals the conflux of two influences: advancement and retrospect, form and 'life', on which we will focus attention in the next chapters. In fact these two streams of influence are constantly crossing and countering one another, setting up not so much a dialectic, as the rhythm of movement and countermovement, systole and diastole which one would expect of a work entitled *The Waves*. This movement is pervasive, and affects the character of the entire work – one of the main reasons for its sometimes disturbing fluidity. With such preliminary soundings to guide us, let us now attempt to confront that fluid texture of the work itself in a more detailed and searching analysis.

Chapter 2

Intention

The place to begin analysis of *The Waves* is to examine the intentions which lay behind the work. Establishing what Virginia Woolf thought she was doing, what her aims and ambitions were (insofar as they are revealed to us), will take us some way toward explaining the peculiarities of the book's form and begin to unravel some of the knotty difficulties of its meaning. Fortunately, Woolf left behind a great repository of comment on her hopes and fears for art in her voluminous diary. Now published in its full form, this diary has become an invaluable resource for the student, and in its pages we can begin to establish the lines of thought which lay behind this strange work.

Continuity and interruption: *Orlando*

One of the first and in many ways most important things which the diary makes plain is that the inspiration which was eventually to develop into *The Waves* came to her in late 1926, when she was in the last stages of writing her fifth novel, *To the Lighthouse*. We will come to the precise nature of this inspiration presently, but first it is worth pausing on the mere fact of this coincidence. There are many structural and thematic links between the two works, so in one sense this juxtaposition is satisfying. But it is also problematic and puzzling; for the book which followed *To the Lighthouse* was not in fact *The Waves*, but *Orlando*, a work which is radically different from either — and indeed different from anything else Woolf ever wrote. Charting the development of *The Waves* therefore demands that we sort out the tangled relation to its two predecessors, and establish the genuine lines of continuity in its evolution.

To the Lighthouse has often been seen as Virginia Woolf's greatest artistic success, and certainly at the time she herself thought so. While retyping the final draft of the novel she recorded her opinion that it was 'easily the best of my books . . . freer & subtler' than any previous effort (23 Nov. 1926). And indeed the general critical consensus has been that in this work Woolf not only perfected her fictional technique, entering the 'luminous halo' of consciousness with greater freedom and flexibility than ever before, but also put her 'method' to greatest artistic purpose. Such success has often been explained by the fact that *To the Lighthouse* was based on deeply biographical material, Woolf's cherished memories and complicated feelings toward her parents and childhood. While there was some struggle in coming to terms with these experiences, there is no doubt that the effort of grappling with this difficult and deeply buried subject left her feeling she had made great gains in her art. In this same diary entry she writes that her own fictional 'method' may have been made perfect through the effort, and now be ready to 'serve whatever use I wish to put it to'. She had no immediate idea as to what that use might be, but casting about for something to follow she records a sense of being 'haunted by some semi-mystic very profound life of a woman, which shall all be told on one occassion; & time shall be utterly obliterated'. In retrospect, this is clearly discernible as the first version of *The Waves*, know as *The Moths*. The point to be grasped here is that the initial impulse of *The Waves* followed hard on the heels of *To the Lighthouse*, rising out of the momentous swell of triumph and success which that novel produced.

Normally when Woolf had the conception of a new work in sight she pursued it vigorously, to the end. Indeed there are signs that she was starting to develop 'these mystical feelings' as she called them through the early part of 1927. Yet in this case something intervened. She suddenly turned sharply away from this course and set off on quite a different tack. This abrupt change of direction, and the reasons for it, were clearly signalled in her diary entry for 14 March 1927:

. . . the truth is I feel the need of an escapade after these serious
poetic experimental books whose form is always so closely
considered. I want to kick up my heels & be off . . . I think this will
be great fun to write; & it will rest my head before starting the very
serious, mystical poetical work which I want to come next.

Much later Woolf returned to this entry and annotated it
'*Orlando* leading to *The Waves*'. It is of course with that
'serious, mystical poetical work' which came next that we are
most directly concerned. However, before treating this
further it will be helpful to fix more clearly the nature of that
'escapade' which forestalled its composition.

Orlando (1928) cannot be reckoned as one of Woolf's
major works, a fact of which she herself was perfectly aware.
As we see, before it is fully conceived she thought of the book
as 'an escapade', something which would be 'fun to write';
and after it was finished she spoke of it in similar terms: 'I
have written this book quicker than any; & it is all a joke .
. . a writer's holiday' (18 March 1928). This 'joke' was a free-
wheeling fantasy which took its eponymous hero/ine through
400 years of English history (predominantly literary history),
with a sex change halfway through. She did indeed 'kick up
her heels' in this book, a work of high, free spirits, fuelled on
the exuberance of her love affair with Vita Sackville-West, on
whom the heroine is based, and who supplied several
photographs for the first edition. Woolf makes clear,
furthermore, both in letters and diary, that the sub-text of the
work was Vita's struggle to retain possession of her ancestral
home of Knole. In essence *Orlando* was a prolonged love-
letter to Vita, and because of this the book has lately received
a good deal of attention from feminist critics, eager to invest
the slight production with more weight than it can bear. But
Woolf herself never suffered under any such illusions; to the
end the book was for her the product of an 'overmastering
impulse' for 'fun'. She refers to it with remarkable
consistency throughout its brief appearance in her diary: in
addition to being 'an escapade' and 'a joke', she describes it
as 'a treat', 'a farce', and 'a fantasy', not to be confused with
her more serious and taxing efforts. The most telling

comment along these lines came after *Orlando* was finished and she began to turn her thoughts to the future:

Orlando is of course a very quick brilliant book. Yes, but I did not try to explore. And must I always explore? Yes I think so still . . . Orlando taught me how to write a direct sentence; taught me continuity & narrative & how to keep the realities at bay. But I purposely avoided of course any other difficulty. I never got down to my depths & made shapes square up, as I did in The Lighthouse.
(7 Nov. 1928)

This extract crystallizes and clarifies the meaning of the term 'holiday' which she used to describe the work; the production of *Orlando* was literally a vacation, a break from the more serious and sustained engagements of her art. Written with tremendous freedom and verve, the book was a product of what she sometimes called her 'upper mind', that superficial layer of intelligence responsible for her sprightliness and wit in company, which informs her dashing letters and inspires her presence at social occasions. (It is significant that she thought the 'sparkling, urgent' vein indulged in *Orlando* was 'stimulated by applause'.) What this meant is effectively recognized in the diary entry above, namely that the deeper, more serious level of Woolf's imagination was not engaged in the book. Getting down into her 'depths' to 'explore' those solitary and subconscious reaches of the mind was an altogether more difficult undertaking and a daunting prospect. To make 'shapes square up' was to make that attempt, to try and fit vision to design – an extreme effort for Woolf, precisely that 'exacting form of intercourse' she had depicted in Lily Briscoe's exhausting struggle with her painting in *To the Lighthouse*. Clearly she decided she needed a rest before undertaking that effort again, and *Orlando* was that holiday. But it is equally clear that, after the holiday was over, she was preparing to get back down to work.

What this perspective makes clear is that *Orlando* was in every sense of the word a diversion for Virginia Woolf. Planned as something which would be 'fun to write', the book represented a respite wherein she could 'rest her head' before starting that serious mystical work which was to come next. This was of course *The Waves*, and when considering its gestation and development it is important to recognize that the deeper, underlying continuity is with *To the Lighthouse*. Both were 'serious poetic experimental books' whose form had to be closely considered. This brings us to the first major strand of Woolf's intention in *The Waves*, which is to resume her serious formal experimentation. To 'explore' here clearly means to explore the bounds of form; to make 'shapes square up' is to push technical innovation in new directions. After the break she clearly resolved to return to the formal exploration she had pursued since the beginning of the decade, to renew and extend that modernist programme of development she had left off in *To the Lighthouse*.

Indeed if anything the hiatus made her more determined than ever to engage in changing the shape of fiction, a fact which helps to account for the virulence of her attacks on the concept of the novel about this time. Upon completing *Orlando* she noted in her diary: 'I feel more & more sure that I will never write a novel again' (18 March, 1928); and two months later, after despatching the manuscript to the printer, she observed: 'I'm glad to be quit this time of writing "a novel"; & hope never to be accused of it again' (31 May 1928). As we shall see, the struggle against 'the novel' was by no means an easy one, and offers a recurrent theme in the book. A reflection of this can be seen at one point in the draft manuscript of *The Waves*, where she inserted in the margin a directive to the effect that 'the author would be glad if the following pages were not read as a novel'. By far the most vehement and indicative statement on this point, however, occurred later in the year when she was well into the first version of *The Waves* (then still called *The Moths*):

The idea has come to me that what I want now to do is to saturate every atom. I mean to eliminate all waste, deadness, superfluity: to give the moment whole; whatever it includes. Say that the moment is a combination of thought; sensation; the voice of the sea. Waste, deadness, come from the inclusion of things that dont belong to the moment; this appalling narrative business of the realist: getting on from lunch to dinner: it is false, unreal, merely conventional. Why admit any thing to literature that is not poetry – by which I mean saturated? Is that not my grudge against novelists? that they select nothing? The poets succeeding by simplifying: practically everything is left out. I want to put practically everything in; yet to saturate. That is what I want to do in The Moths.   (28 Nov. 1928)

There is a great deal in this extract which bears on the form of *The Waves*, which we will examine in due course; but what holds our interest here is the strength of the attack on the 'conventional' matter of the novel. Her slating of 'this appalling narrative business of the realist' has a virulence which may remind us of the tone of her earlier essay, 'Modern Fiction', from which I quoted above. This in itself is puzzling; for at the beginning of the decade she badly needed to clear imaginative space for herself, and her attack on the Edwardian 'realists', Bennett and Wells, was part of a necessary intellectual strategy; here, after several successful and highly experimental works there was no similar pressing need. However, it may have been the nature of *Orlando* itself which sharpened this edge. This explosion in the diary, like the other comments about being quit of 'the novel', have a distinctly defensive air about them, which was probably caused by that work's highly conventional nature. For all its fantastic elements 'keeping realities at bay', *Orlando* essentially abandoned the luminous innovative technique she had been developing throughout the decade. It was a work of 'direct sentences', of 'continuity & narrative', and this was evidently to counter the difficulty and obscurity of her own 'method'. 'I am writing *Orlando* half in a mock style very clear & plain, so that people will understand every word', she wrote (22 Oct. 1927). In fact the book returns to many of the 'novelistic' conventions she had previously foresworn – third-person narration through an omniscient narrator, a highly plotted story unfolding in linear progression – and this fact undoubtedly made the modernist side of Virginia Woolf nervous. Hence her determination to redouble her attack on conventional forms of fiction as she emerged from *Orlando* and embarked on her next book.

Here then is the first clue to *The Waves*. It is clear that in returning from her 'holiday' in 1928 to pick up on the threads of that mystical, poetical work, Woolf was deliberately setting out to renew and revitalize the strain of formal experiment and technical innovation which had inspired all her serious work since 1919. Behind the closely considered form of the 'serious poetic experimental' work she eventually produced lies a resumption of the formalist impulse which took her beyond the 'merely conventional' notions of fiction and produced her great modern novels, *Mrs Dalloway* and *To the Lighthouse*.

'These mystical feelings'

Part of the extreme strangeness of *The Waves*, then, results from the resumption of what we might call her modernist impulse, her renewed resolve to push the form of fiction beyond its customary and conventional compass. Working in tandem with this formalist drive, however, was another impulse whose sources were wholly different – deeper and more difficult to extricate. This second strand of intention also surfaced as Woolf was completing *To the Lighthouse*, recorded in a diary entry which most observers have taken to represent the origin of *The Waves*.

I wished to add some remarks to this, on the mystical side of this solitude; how it is not oneself but something in the universe that one's left with. It is this that is frightening & exciting in the midst of my profound gloom, depression, boredon, whatever it is: One sees a fin passing far out. What image can I reach to convey what I mean? Really there is none I think. The interesting thing is that in all my feeling & thinking I have never come up against this before. Life is, soberly & accurately, the oddest affair; has in it the essence of reality. I used to feel this as a child – couldn't step across a puddle once I remember, for thinking, how strange – what am I? etc. . . . All I mean to make is a note of a curious state of mind. I hazard the guess that it may be the impulse behind another book. At present my mind is totally blank and virgin of books.

(30 Sept. 1926)

Such an opaque and orphic entry might not seem of much help, but for Woolf the experience it records was crucially connected with *The Waves*. In October 1929, after *Orlando* was long over and she was well into work on the book, she returned to this entry and annotated her hazard as 'Perhaps The Waves or moths'. More importantly, in the immediate exultation and relief of completing her final draft she recorded her feeling that she had 'netted that fin in the waste of waters which appeared to me over the marshes out of my window at Rodmell when I was coming to an end of *To the Lighthouse*' (7 Feb. 1931). Clearly this entry was of seminal importance, and in some way persisted throughout the course of the book's development. I want, in the following pages, to examine this entry with some care, and will refer to it throughout as the 'origin' or 'originating entry' of *The Waves*.

Perhaps the most striking thing about this entry is its haziness — it recounts a vague mood, 'a curious state of mind' barely imaged in the fin passing far out. This is striking because it affords such a contrast to the moments of inspiration for other books recorded in the diary. At one point after completing *To the Lighthouse*, she suddenly lept up with the idea of 'a biography beginning in the year 1500 & continuing to the present day, called *Orlando*: Vita; only with a change about from one sex to another' (5 Oct. 1927). All the salient features of the book are here, even to the title; the inspiration came to her 'instantly' and entire. The same is true of the serious, poetic, experimental work which preceded it:

I'm now all on the strain with desire to . . . get on to *To the Lighthouse*. This is going to be fairly short: to have father's character done complete in it; & mother's; & St Ives; & childhood; & all the usual things I try to put in — life, death, etc. But the centre is father's character, sitting in a boat, reciting we perished, each alone, while he crushes a dying mackarel.   (14 May 1925)

The clear, coherent image, with associated themes swarming about it, seems to hold the entire book complete, in a nutshell. The contrast with the diffuse and vague origin of *The Waves* quoted above could not be greater. And significantly, while she wrote both these works quickly, expanding the compacted germ of the conception, the evolution of *The*

Waves proved a far slower and more difficult process, 'nothing like the speed & certainty of the *Lighthouse*: *Orlando* mere child's play' (2 Nov. 1929). All of which suggests that the vagueness and insubstantiality of the conception was taking her in a new direction, charting deeper and more difficult waters than any she had explored before.

The originating diary entry of September 30 does offer us some clues as to the direction in which she was moving, the first one contained in that seemingly innocuous phrase, 'not oneself'. This is revealing because one of the persistent fears which dogged her exploration of the 'luminous halo' of consciousness was becoming imprisoned in the subjective. When first beginning to evolve her distinctive 'method' she recorded her feeling that 'the danger is the damned egotistical self; which ruins Joyce & [Dorothy] Richardson to my mind'. Like Keats she had an aversion to the egotistical sublime, and yet she had not been able to detach herself completely from her art. The sources behind both *To the Lighthouse* and *Orlando* were personal, and it is highly indicative that she repeatedly worried over the fact that *To the Lighthouse* would be thought 'sentimental'. After the book was completed Woolf recorded her wish to 'forget one's own sharp absurd little personality' and to 'practise anonymity' − a desire which was to be put to pointed effect in *The Waves*; writing to John Lehmann after the book was finished, she said: 'I wanted to eliminate all detail, all fact . . . & myself.' The purge of fictional material was linked to a purge of the self, and here one can begin to see why she expunged her first conception of a shadowy female narrator ('telling the story on one occasion') and allowed the characters to usurp the narrative function themselves; as we shall see the narrator was too difficult to disentangle from herself. What is of paramount importance here is to note that the initial impulse behind *The Waves* was immediately linked with something that was 'not oneself' but something more universal. This gives us the first indication that in this work Woolf was attempting to move 'beyond personality', pushing her fiction out toward a more impersonal and anonymous stage.

Well, we might ask, what in the universe *is* one left with?
— a question which compels us to investigate this cryptic
passage more closely and to try and describe its effect. The
dominant impression of the entry is one of mental musing
which borders on the abstract, imbued with qualities of the
impersonal and remote. (Subsequently attempting to flesh out
this conception, she noted the work might be told by 'a mind
thinking'.) The key phrases which convey this meditative and
'mystical' aspect are 'something in the universe that one's left
with' and 'the essence of reality', both of which suggest an
element of brooding, impersonal abstraction. This notion is
reinforced by the diary entry which immediately follows,
where she extends this air of strange deliberation: 'once or
twice & very vaguely', she writes, she has attempted 'a
dramatisation of my mood at Rodmell. It is to be an
endeavour at something mystical, spiritual; the thing that
exists when we aren't there' (30 Oct. 1926). Such hints
consolidate the 'mystical' direction in which she was moving,
but are not in themselves terribly clear. She was diverted by
Orlando before she could pursue 'these mystical feelings'
much further; but after the 'escapade' was over she returned
to them and began to enlarge on what she meant. One entry
in the late summer of 1928 seems particularly relevant:

This has been a very animated summer: a summer lived almost too
much in public. Often down here [Rodmell] I have entered a
sanctuary; a nunnery; had a religious retreat; of great agony once;
& always some terror: so afraid is one of loneliness: of seeing to the
bottom of the vessel. That is one of the experiences I have had in
some Augusts; & got then to a consciousness of what I call 'reality':
a thing I see before me; something abstract; but residing in the
downs or sky; beside which nothing matters; in which I shall rest &
continue to exist. Reality I call it. And I fancy sometimes this is the
most necessary thing to me: that which I seek.   (10 Sept. 1928)

This entry represents a considerable expansion on the
'mystical' 'spiritual' sense of 'the thing that exists when we
aren't there'. 'Reality' she calls it, and this 'abstract' element
is clearly gesturing toward some 'religious' or metaphysical
element, even though it is not otherworldly but rather a
'natural supernaturalism', residing before her in the Downs

and the sky. This 'consciousness of reality' must be linked with that 'essence of reality' she had perceived before, and it provides a clear indication of the direction in which Woolf's thoughts were moving at this time − away from personal and social concerns towards larger, more abstract and philosophical issues of being, the 'oddity' and strangeness of life and the mysteries of identity ('what am I? etc.'). This was the direction in which Virginia Woolf was to take *The Waves*, but to complete our tracing of the intentions behind the work we must follow one final clue in the diary entry above, contained in the phrase 'that which I seek'. For though she occasionally senses this enlarged and essential aspect of 'reality', it is evidently not always present to her but rather something she searches for. And this idea of seeking it directs us to yet another diary entry, where she makes the matter clearer. In fact Woolf was not wholly accurate in saying she had never come up against the feeling before, for earlier in the same year she had recorded a highly suggestive rumination in her diary which recapitulates her apprehension of 'something in the universe that one's left with':

Mrs Webb's book has made me think a little what I could say of my own life . . . there were causes in her life: prayer, principle. None in mine. Great excitability & search after something. Great content − almost always enjoying what I'm at, but with constant change of mood . . . I enjoy almost everything. Yet I have some restless searcher in me. Why is there not a discovery in life? Something one can lay hands on & say 'This is it'? My depression is a harassed feeling − I'm looking; but that's not it − that's not it. What is it? And shall I die before I find it? Then (as I was walking through Russell Square last night) I see the mountains in the sky: the great clouds; & the moon which is risen over Persia; I have a great & astonishing sense of something there, which is 'it' − It is not exactly beauty that I mean. It is that the thing is in itself enough: satisfactory; achieved. A sense of my own strangeness, walking on the earth is there too: of the infinite oddity of the human position; trotting along Russell Square with the moon up there and those mountain clouds. Who am I, what am I, & so on: these questions are always floating about in me . . .   (27 Feb. 1926)

This passage also works toward the suggestion of 'something in the universe that one's left with', but it adds to this the sense of Woolf as a 'restless searcher', actively looking for 'some discovery in life' and finding it in odd moments. As we shall see, this is actually much closer to the sense and feel of *The Waves* than the previous two entries, but it points in the same direction, namely toward the abstract, speculative and philosophical side of Virginia Woolf. What is suggested here is an epistemological quest, a search for the Kantian *Ding an sich*, a clarified apprehension of 'the thing itself' which will yield a new knowledge of reality. 'It' for which she searches here is clearly commensurate with that mysterious 'essence of reality' she described in seeing the fin passing far out later that year, and coming upon it in odd moments of transfigured being yields a feeling of completion and content similar to the apprehension of 'reality' in the Downs or sky. All of these entries illustrate the abstract or philosophical direction in which she was now moving, focusing on those 'essential' questions which were always floating about in her.

This last phrase cautions us not to exaggerate the novelty of this development, and indeed for the attentive reader of Woolf's work the theme of seeking a true knowledge of reality may begin to suggest links with previous novels: 'What is the meaning of life? That was all – a simple question; one that tended to close in on one with years'. Lily Briscoe's plangent question as she sets up her painting in the third section of *To the Lighthouse* reminds us that the feelings which would animate *The Waves* have not been entirely absent from Woolf's work hitherto (indeed the notion of 'the thing that exists when we aren't there' had been identified by Andrew Ramsay as the subject of his father's researches: 'Think of a kitchen table when you're not there'). Here is the first of many indications that her 'completely new attempt' would not be as new as she thought, and that previous novels, especially *To the Lighthouse*, will form a guide to the mysteries of *The Waves*. But what the diary does make plain is that such questioning was now coming to the fore in a more apparent way, revealing a clarified metaphysical impulse. Lily's wish to know 'the meaning of life' was still operative and would inform *The Waves*, but, as we might expect,

Woolf's 'new attempt' would shift towards a more generalized and 'essential' search for that meaning.

We may now begin to understand that obscure impulse behind the origin of *The Waves* and thus to establish the second strand of her intentions in the work. Various critics have pointed to the 'radically contemplative' nature of this originating entry, and its aspect of serious and deliberate thought would have considerable impact on the final work. The years had clearly brought Virginia Woolf to the philosophic mind. With the past success of personal exploration behind her, she was now moving towards a more abstract and philosophical contemplation of life, endeavouring to come to grips with 'the essence of reality' it contained. *The Waves* was to be the forum in which she would engage in the restless search for 'it', undertaking a serious metaphysical quest for the universal and fundamental aspect of 'reality'. (Indeed while at work on the book she once told Leonard that the book was seeking to explore 'the fundamental things in human existence'.) Though frequently teased by her Cambridge friends for her 'lack of intellectual power', Woolf was sufficiently her father's daughter to want, in her own unsystematic way, to engage in 'philosophy' (though serious thinkers may blanch at the term), at least to the extent of offering some thrust at an essential vision of life. Indeed the very phrase 'the essence of reality' has more than a slight reasonance of G. E. Moore, the Cambridge philosopher whose method of stripping to the essential had such an impact on Bloomsbury. In any event, we mistake *The Waves* if we do not see this 'metaphysical' impulse joining her modernist one at the outset. As an aside we may note that the investigation of 'reality' in this way is part of a larger current of modernism itself, visible for instance in T. S. Eliot's disctum that 'human kind cannot bear very much reality', or in Wallace Stevens's efforts to reach 'a new knowledge of reality'. This notion of a search for some essential, abstract principle of being within the contexts of human life can also be found in such writers as Yeats, Lawrence and Joyce, as well as in continental figures such as Rilke and Valery.

From this point of view *The Waves* resolves itself into Virginia Woolf's most ambitious book, her attempt to 'reach into the silence' after some abstract and universal principle in human life. Put more briefly, *The Waves*, that serious, mystical, experimental book to come next, was to be nothing less than her attempt to express 'reality'. In this work she would endeavour to 'come to terms with these mystical feelings', to convey that perception she experienced on some occasions of 'something in the universe that one's left with'. 'Reality' as she called it was thus not to be confused with realism, that appalling narrative business of giving the conventional forms and thickened textures of appearance; rather it was meant to signify 'the essence of reality', the 'fundamental' core of mere being. Such vague and unrealized notions may give some idea why she had such a struggle in this book to make 'shapes square up' to her vision. At any rate it is clear that Woolf was indeed turning back to her 'depths' as she embarked on *The Waves*, perhaps sounding more deeply ('to the bottom of the vessel') than ever before. Her earlier efforts to purge the novel of its casual and encrusted form were now joined to the search for an 'abstract' conception of life which went beyond personal effects and the particulars of biography. Form would follow function, as mysticism and modernism meet in the fluent texture of *The Waves*.

Chapter 3

Form

Poetry, prose, drama

To sum up the preceding discussion, Virginia Woolf's intentions as she began work on *The Waves* were at once to resume her formal experimentation, with its implied attack on the realistic novel, and to undertake philosophical investigations, searching for some metaphysical principle which transcended the local and personal interests of her previous work. The next 'serious poetic experimental' book was to be one in which modernism and mysticism would meet. What then, we may ask, were the formal consequences of these ambitions? How was she to adjust her technique to encompass these twin aims? These were questions which perplexed Woolf herself a good deal, and she was a long time in finding an answer. The prolonged gestation of *The Waves* and the false trail she followed in its initial version, *The Moths*, is a study unto itself — a study much facilitated by the labours of J. W. Graham, who has capably edited the two versions. (Students interested in this 'archeological' aspect of the work are referred to Graham's edition. Our concern is with the finished product, and consequently I focus on *The Waves* itself in this discussion, making reference to the earlier conception as needed to elucidate the final work.) As we shall see, the answer she finally found was extremely different from anything she had produced before, and these differences make themselves most keenly felt on the level of form, which, as she indicated, was now to be 'closely considered'.

As usual, it is the diary which provides the first indications of what shape these ambitions were to take. Though immediately after the strange inspiration at Rodmell she made vague attempts to 'dramatise her mood', it was not until the following year that she made the first tentative and suggestive efforts to flesh out the conception, with the following bold entry:

Why not invent a new kind of play — as for instance
Woman thinks: . . .
He does.
Organ Plays.
She writes.
They say:
She sings:
Night speaks:
They miss   (21 Feb. 1927)

I quote this extract not because it does Woolf any justice; she
was clearly sketching out a rudimentary idea here, as she
often did in her diary, and perhaps the best one can say of this
curiously meaningless *mélange* is that she did not pursue it.
Yet in these bare subjects and predicates we see an urge to
generalize and abstract which is in line with the tenor of her
thinking at this time. What is most revealing in this extract,
however, is the way it suddenly reaches out to dramatic form;
her attempt to push beyond the normal bounds of fiction
turns her in the direction of a play. She concludes the entry:
'I think it must be something in this line — though I cant now
see what. Away from facts: free; yet concentrated; prose yet
poetry; a novel & a play.' The desire to combine prose and
poetry recapitulates her previous aesthetic ideals and stylistic
achievements, what she called 'my lyric vein'; but she has
added to this the new idea of merging a novel and a play.
A year later, after *Orlando* was over, she returned to this
idea: and the novel combination clearly has caught her
imagination: 'Yes but *The Moths*? That was to be an abstract
mystical eyeless book: a playpoem' (7 Nov. 1928). Here we
see form following function as it is the 'abstract' and
'mystical' effort which leads to the formal idea of a
'playpoem'.
   These incipient suggestions in the diary are considerably
enlarged in the more expansive form of a critical essay,
something Woolf was wont to do on the verge of a new
formal development. This work, one of the key documents
for studying *The Waves*, was originally delivered as a lecture
at Oxford in May 1927, entitled 'Poetry, Fiction and the
Future', and subsequently published in her *Collected Essays*

as 'The Narrow Bridge of Art'. Here Woolf speculated at length on future shape of fiction, and in the process provided a considerable guide to the direction her thoughts were taking at this time. Briefly summarized, her argument is as follows: the modern age is one of 'doubt and conflict', wherein 'all bonds of union seem broken', leaving the problem for the creative artist to express this sense of division and discord yet at the same time assert some power of harmony and control. Such difficulties have bested most efforts of modern literature, which is divided, blocked and frustrated in its attempt to express the full sense of 'life'. In particular, she singles out 'the failure of poetry' to fulfil its tasks as before. Modern poetry, she says, is persistently one-sided, aware of the ugliness and incongruity of life, but unable to combine this with beauty; thus it cannot bring the whole of life together in harmony. This failure is particularly revealed in the inability to create a modern poetic play. While the age abounds with lyric poetry, with its lovely cries of ecstasy or despair, it has been unable to deal with the comprehensive dramatic form. Such efforts as have been made are stilted, awkward, and self-conscious, invariably set in the past and thus avoiding the challenge of the present day. She contrasts this with the ideal form which once did express precisely this sense of confusion and contradiction in a harmonious whole – the poetic drama of the Elizabethan age. Then the 'poetic play' had been vital and alive, fully capable of dealing with contemporary life; it had been a form able 'to express an attitude which is full of contrast and collision' demanding 'the conflict of one character upon another' and at the same time offering 'some general shaping power, some conception which lends the whole harmony and force'. There is, she says, none of the contemporary bafflement and frustration in Shakespeare: 'without a hitch he turns from philosophy to a drunken brawl; from love songs to an argument; from simple merriment to profound speculation'. Such artistic confidence and completeness, the power to deal with life as a whole, has vanished from the contemporary scene, thus leaving a lamentable vaccuum in the art of the age.

It is not my purpose here to comment on the justice of Woolf's argument. (She plainly has the poetry of T. S. Eliot in mind though, interestingly enough, this essay was written before Eliot produced any of his plays.) The truth of her claim is less relevant to us than the fact that she is obviously once more trying to clear imaginative space for herself, to suggest or open a new direction for her formal advance. Quite plainly she intends to appropriate for herself, not simply the lyrical intensities of 'poetry', but these combined with the form and function of drama – in short, the poetic play. Indeed she goes on in the essay to make just this claim. Since poetry is now incapable of discharging its time-honoured function, prose must eventually shoulder the poetic tasks, and 'that cannibal, the novel, which has devoured so many forms' will consume another. The fiction of the future, she claims,

will be written in prose, but in prose which has many of the characteristics of poetry. It will have something of the exaltation of poetry, but much of the ordinariness of prose. It will be dramatic, and yet not a play. It will be read, not acted . . . it will differ from the novel as we know it now chiefly in that it will stand further back from life. It will give, as poetry does, the outline rather than the detail. It will make little use of the marvellous fact-recording power, which is one of the attributes of fiction. It will tell us very little about the houses, incomes, occupations of its characters . . . It will resemble poetry in this that it will give not only or mainly people's reactions to each other and their activities together, as the novel has hitherto done, but it will give the relation of the mind to general ideas and its soliloquy in solitude.

Here Woolf outlines the direction of her next formal advance. The form of fiction she has in mind is one which would move away from the 'merely conventional' pattern of the novel as we know it now in order to approach the comprehensive interest, harmonizing power and poetic force of Elizabethan drama. Such a form would shift the emphasis off that 'marvellous fact-recording power' which currently obsesses prose fiction, and place it on the more abstract element of 'general ideas' and a freer, more flexible style. Above all, such a fiction would 'stand further back from life', focusing 'as poetry does, on the outline rather than the detail' – in other words encompassing the general and universal perspectives of life which neither the novel nor the poetry of the day can do. Here we can detect more than an echo of her diary entry which wished to 'eliminate' all waste, deadness and superfluity from fiction. Her whole aim in this extract is to 'concentrate', to 'saturate' the novel with the abstract and essential. The form she sketches out here is fully in accord with her expressed intentions.

This passage represents a considerable expansion of Woolf's diary suggestions about combining poetry and prose, the novel and the play, and it is the clearest indication we have of the way in which she was to move in her next serious, experimental work. For here in a nutshell are many of the salient formal features of *The Waves*. Once we grasp this strange union of powers as her over-riding ambition, we shall be less startled and troubled by the shock of our first venture into that work.

'I see a ring,' said Bernard, 'hanging above me. It quivers and hangs in a loop of light.'

'I see a slab of pale yellow,' said Susan, 'spreading away until it meets a purple stripe.'

'I hear a sound,' said Rhoda, 'cheep, chirp; cheep, chirp; going up and down.'

'I see a globe,' said Neville, 'hanging down in a drop against the enormous flanks of some hill.'

'I see a crimson tassel,' said Jinny, 'twisted with gold threads.'

'I hear something stamping,' said Louis. 'A great beast's foot is chained. It stamps, and stamps, and stamps.'

'Look at the spider's web on the corner of the balcony,' said Bernard. 'It has beads of water on it, drops of white light.'

'The leaves are gathered round the window like pointed ears,' said Susan.

'A shadow falls on the path,' said Louis, 'like an elbow bent.'

'Islands of light are swimming on the grass,' said Rhoda. 'They have fallen through the trees.'

'The birds eyes are bright in the tunnels between the leaves,' said Neville.

'The stalks are covered with harsh, short hairs,' said Jinny, 'and drops of water have stuck to them.'

These speeches introduce the six figures who dominate *The Waves*, and the strange form of conscious declamation which continues throughout the work. We can see at once how the writing attempts to fulfil Woolf's aims; though written in prose it has many of the characteristics of lyric poetry – an arch, elevated style, an incantatory rhythm and, increasingly, a suffusion of simile and metaphor. Yet, for all that, the prose is remarkably 'ordinary', the diction simple, often colloquial, avoiding elaborate or latinate sonorities. It is writing which, in a curious way, hovers between poetry and prose, as Woolf intended. Moreover, we are not likely to think of this as the opening of a 'novel', as the narrator has disappeared, leaving the characters to speak their parts in a strange manner approaching dramatic form. Woolf's own term for the speeches was 'soliloquies', indicating her borrowing from the drama and the absence of dialogue in the work suggests that 'soliloquy in solitude' she wished to convey. Yet this is clearly not a play, meant to be read rather than acted, as indicated through the sustained narrative devices of quotation marks and the verb 'said' which appears throughout. Once again the writing seems to hover between forms. On first approach, *The Waves* suggests a strange and wonderful fusion of formal energies, a combination of the novel, poetry and the play – precisely the hybrid she wished to create.

It is small wonder that Woolf called *The Waves* 'this ecstatic book' and thought of it as 'my first work in my own style'. Certainly the work is very different, in a number of ways, from anything she ever did before; but this very novelty has had its pitfalls. Readers comfortable with Woolf's previous fiction are understandably baffled, not to say shocked, at the spectacle of a work which stands so aloof from the traditional form of the novel, and which reverses so much of her past achievements. There is a rare unanimity among critics, all of whom comment on the way in which this book departs from the 'luminous' interiority and subjective style of Woolf's earlier novels, whether or not they like the change. It is worth pausing to explore just what some of these changes are.

Perhaps the most immediately striking difference from Woolf's previous work is that the characters are perpetually speaking: their every appearance is externalized through the convention of direct, reported speech. The effect is remarkable because speech had been so effectively subdued before. When we open *Mrs Dalloway* or *To the Lighthouse*, we immediately plunge to the centre of the character's mental world, a rapid whirl of perception, memory, emotion and thought which scarcely ever breaks the surface in direct speech. Woolf's aesthetic goals, and her 'method' so painstakingly developed through the Twenties, had been purposely devised to 'look within', plunging into the 'luminous halo' of the mind so as to examine the interstices of consciousness. Her wish had been to capture 'the flickerings of that innermost flame which flashes its messages through the brain', depicting the barely conscious workings of the mind as it encounters the world; and the result in her work had been that a character's sub- or semi-conscious motives, desires, pains, pleasures and concerns had been effectively dramatized. Here in *The Waves*, by contrast, such interior levels of awareness disappear; they have been brought to the surface, analyzed and expressed. She has, as it were, inverted her previous technique, and transformed the silent workings of mental process into overt awareness which the characters baldly announce. At a stroke the intricacies of the luminous halo of consciousness have been turned into an extreme form of self-consciousness.

Such a change, however, was clearly signalled in 'The Narrow Bridge of Art', which reveals a sharp reversal in the direction of Woolf's aesthetic theory. No longer is she impatient to enter the 'semi-transparent envelope' of subjective awareness, or urging fiction to focus on the 'incessant shower of innumerable atoms' of sensation, so as to be able to 'trace the pattern . . . which each sight or incident scores upon the consciousness'. Instead she now counsels a withdrawal, pressing fiction to 'stand further back from life' so as to apprehend its general outline. The shift is from a concentration on minute particulars of experience to a concern with larger, more general perspectives. It is, in other words, a shift toward abstraction, one which is in line with those intentions explored in the previous section. A more distanced and detached view is one which will on the one hand call more attention to overall form, and on the other facilitate the exploration of larger, more universal significance. Rather than getting immersed in particular and local detail, the work will be free to focus on more expansive and general concerns.

In effect we can say that thought, conveyed *as thought*, virtually disappears from *The Waves*, and the import of the change is to work against the illusion of felt life. The point is often made that Woolf's previous experimentation had been pursued in aid of a greater naturalism: 'is life like this?' she had asked in 'Modern Fiction', confronting and challenging the excessive focus on surface appearance in the conventional novel of her day. The form of fiction then had been faulted for not being 'realistic' enough, that is to say for failing to give a true and accurate picture of human experience with its 'incessant shower' of sensation. In *The Waves*, however, this ideal has gone; naturalism is clearly beside the point in such a stylized and artificial device as the characters' incessant speech. Among other things this results in a sharp loss in verisimilitude. Hermione Lee has finely observed that the work's refusal to penetrate beneath the conscious level of awareness sacrifices the dramatic tension Woolf had achieved before. The sort of disjunction between an external, social awareness, and an internal, psychological one which made Clarissa Dalloway's encounter with Peter Walsh or Lily Briscoe's with Mr Ramsay such effective and moving moments of fiction has gone from this work. By the same token, the characters' constant speech serves to distance and disengage the reader as well. Self-consciousness, however fluent, lacks the ease or authority of unconscious revelation, and the confessional declamation of these figures has a certain formality and stiffness which dispels the sense of intimacy we enjoyed with Septimus Smith, Mrs Ramsay or Lily Briscoe. The reader is held off, as it were, transformed from an immediately engaged participant, a 'secret sharer' in the character's consciousness, to a removed spectator, or rather, auditor of awareness. The entire effect is more formalized and remote than any previous work.

Style

The impact of this shift is felt on almost every level of *The Waves*, and almost always contributes toward a reduction of the 'novelistic' aspect of the work, in ways which we shall now examine. What contributes most to the strange purified aspect of the work is undoubtedly the *style* of the characters' incessant speech. The compelling power of the language they use is one of the most extraordinary and enchanting aspects of *The Waves*, and its effects require closer inspection. There is a remarkable ease in their speech, but not a conversational ease. Rather it is a 'high style', making full use of such 'poetic' devices as inversions, repetitions, simile and metaphor, a style which leaps to a plateau above the vernacular and stays there. Yet, paradoxically, it is also curiously effortless, as if meeting no resistance in the actual. The speeches are unhurried, lingered over, giving a sense of distilled purity which can seem monotonous, though the verbal resources are such that it generally does not. The function of this extraordinary style is, of course, to get away from the usual conventions of the novel and take the work closer to 'poetry'. The sustained artificiality of the speech detaches it from detailed, prosaic reality. Once again 'The Narrow Bridge of Art' provides a clear indication of this aim. Poetry, Woolf says, 'has never been used for the common purpose of life'; instead prose has shouldered 'all the dirty work . . . has answered letters, paid bills, written articles' and so forth. 'The penalty it pays for having dispensed with the incantation and the mystery, with rhyme and metre' is that it cannot now 'leap at one spring at the heart of its subject' as poetry does. However, she goes on to say that 'if you free it from the beast-of-burden work which so many novelists necessarily lay upon it, of carrying loads of details, bushels of fact − prose thus treated will show itself capable of rising high from the ground', making that inspired leap to the 'essence' of its subject, and sustaining the intensity of such elevation. It is clear that in *The Waves* she was attempting to do just this, freeing prose from its 'fact-recording power', that novelistic beast-of-burden work, so as to attain such heights.

Many critics have recognized that the primary aspect of the work is style, which perhaps explains why most good criticism of *The Waves* is rooted in stylistic analysis. One of the best of these, and a must for every serious student of *The Waves*, is J. W. Graham's essay, 'Point of View in *The Waves*: Some Services of the Style'. In a penetrating analysis to which I am greatly indebted, Graham observes that the rare pure present tense (I go, I see) is used throughout *The Waves*, rather than the more normal present progressive (I am going). The latter form emphasizes the sense of duration with respect to action, but the unusual grammatical feature of the pure present has the effect of suspending the sense of time with respect to action; and its full-scale use in the book has the effect of removing the characters from direct involvement in the world, of suspending them above the actions they describe. As James Naremore, another capable analyst of the style, puts it: 'these voices seem to inhabit a kind of spirit realm from which . . . they comment on their time-bound selves below'. This does indeed capture the feeling of being immersed in *The Waves*, as the following extract will perhaps show.

'Summer comes, and winter,' said Susan. 'The seasons pass. The pear fills itself and drops from the tree . . . I sit by the fire watching the kettle boil. I see the pear tree through the streaked steam on the window-pane.'

'Sleep, sleep, I croon, whether it is summer or winter, May or November . . . I sing my song by the fire like an old shell murmuring on the beach. Sleep, sleep, I say, warning off with my voice all who rattle milk cans, fire at rooks, shoot rabbits, or in any way bring the shock of destruction near this wicker cradle, laden with soft limbs, curled under a pink coverlet.'

. . .

'I pad about the house all day long in apron and slippers, like my mother who died of cancer . . . When the lark peels high his ring of sound and it falls through the air like an apple paring, I stoop; I feed my baby . . . Sleep, I say, desiring sleep to fall like a blanket of down and cover these weak limbs; . . . making of my own body a hollow, a warm shelter for my child to sleep in. Sleep, I say, sleep.'

Admittedly the temporal edges here are blurred because of the habitual, repetitive quality which these actions possess (and which the speech mimes). Even so, it is apparent how thoroughly the style takes control and effectively separates speaker from action. Collapsing all movement and activity into the pure present removes the sense of felt duration of the actions, and thus suspends the sense of a precise location in time. The result is that a sense of actual participation in the world is diminished; action is effectively reconstituted as speech. Susan, as speaker, seems to be hovering above her actions ('I watch the kettle boil', 'I pad about the house', etc.), giving them careful scrutiny and reporting them in fluent speech. The style effectively lifts her out of direct involvement with the activity she describes, so that she appears to be watching herself from some remote height, as Naremore indicated, and commenting on her activity. This effect is typical. Though in one sense concerned with nothing else, these figures' engagement with reality is held off, dissolved in the stream of reflecting speech. Put another way, we can say that in this book the language dispels the action; their speech puts a barrier between the characters and the world, their fluency distances them from the active heat and passion of life. Some contemporary critics would say this of every work of literature (there cannot be any 'real' action in a text, only words), but our interest here is in the relative effect. The conventions of the ordinary, naturalistic novel are designed to give the illusion of active life, to immerse characters in the world of action and time; and relative to this, the suspension of life in discourse in *The Waves* is extreme, exaggerated and deliberate. This is undoubtedly why some readers find the work, in Frank Kermode's term, 'intolerable'.

Here again, Woolf can be seen as following the course she outlined in 'The Narrow Bridge of Art'. The accentuation of such 'poetic' features as rhythm and metre, assonance and alliteration, is in aid of such an effort, of 'rising high from the ground' so as to give, 'as poetry does, the outline rather than the detail' – a feature which has been often observed, though rarely explored. Graham, for example, notes that the style of *The Waves* approximates that of 'the speaker in lyric poetry', but does not elaborate on this. It is true that the style of the speaking portions of the book does echo the effect of much lyric verse, e.g.: 'I cannot see what flowers are at my feet' (Keats), or 'I fall upon the thorns of life; I bleed' (Shelley). I quote examples from the Romantics because a reference to Keats in 'The Narrow Bridge of Art' suggests that this is the 'poetry' she has in mind. But there are other examples closer to her: 'I smile, of course, and go on drinking tea'; 'I know the voices dying with a dying fall / Beneath the music from a farther room'; 'In the room the women come and go / Talking of Michelangelo'. These examples from the early work of T. S. Eliot (a palpable influence on *The Waves*) use the pure present to much the same effect as the Romantics; that is, to engender a split between action and awareness. It is the element of close self-scrutiny, the intensified awareness which reflects a solitary, meditating mind which all these poets seek to convey. It is for precisely the same use, the 'soliloquy in solitude', that Woolf appropriates the device in *The Waves*. Her aim is similarly to shift the emphasis from action to awareness of action, from experience of life to reflection and analysis. The *meditative* pressure in the speeches of *The Waves* is enormous, and largely the result of the style. The effect is compounded by the highly artificial 'poeticism' of the language – its lulling, alliterative cadences (in this last extract – 'Sleep, sleep, I croon . . .' – meant to mime the lullaby), and its 'saturation' in metaphor. (Susan's likening to 'an old shell murmuring on the beach' is a good example, in this case preparing for the subsequent metaphor of 'making my own body a hollow' in which the child shelters.) While this highly self-conscious speech becomes so much a part of the usual mode of the book that it hardly ever seems out of place, the cumulative effect is undeniable: the artificiality of the language separates the speaker from the events described, emphasizing a reflecting and composing consciousness, a mental state above the material plane of existence. In sum, all these accentuated effects of style compound the static and unnatural effect, thus helping to displace the book from the time-bound, active, engaged sense of 'the novel'.

Character

A related consequence of such stylistic displacement is to diminish the traditional notion of 'character'. In fact the six figures of *The Waves* remain almost wholly generalized; none of them, for instance, has any placing surname, and details of their past are kept to a minimum. We know that Louis has an Australian accent, that his father is a banker in Brisbane, but little more, and the others have even less background. Moreover, as they grow and develop, the personal fabric of their lives remains sketchy at best: Bernard marries and has a son, Susan's farmer husband gives her many children, Neville and Jinny have a number of love affairs, and so on; but these relations are revealed in asides and effectively remain outside the focus of the book. By the same token, the settings are kept uniformly generalized; instead of the definite, locating details of Mrs Dalloway's journey through London, the surroundings here are kept vague, suggestive rather than precise. Nothing which might root them too firmly in a substantial or definite identity is allowed to intrude, and Forster's comment about their being 'wraiths' has some force.

One technical feature which increases this effect is the absence of the narrator, that staple device of the novel. One of the traditional resources of fiction has been the ability of narrative to impart additional information and so enrich the reader's grasp and understanding of character. The novelist has traditionally used the bridging narrative sections between dialogue to flesh out the background history, psychological make-up, relevant emotional idiosyncrasies and quirks of his characters. When, for instance, in the opening chapter of George Eliot's *Middlemarch* the narrator says of the heroine,

'Her mind was theoretic, and yearned by its nature after some lofty conception of the world', our understanding of Dorothea Brooke, and of the action which ensues, is greatly enhanced. Similarly the comment at the outset of *The Ambassadors* that 'There was detachment in his zeal and curiosity in his indifference' helps the reader form an assessment of Lambert Strether which qualifies our perception of his mission. Virginia Woolf had in fact refined this narrative ability to a highly developed point of subtlety and precision, as Auerbach has shown, offering a great deal of enriching and focusing comment which appeared to emanate from a strange, unlocatable source, close to but not within the characters themselves. Yet in *The Waves* such diagetical resource is abandoned. The characters themselves usurp the narrative function; the information about them is provided at the level of conscious awareness. This has other effects, while we will examine later, but for the moment it is sufficient to observe that though they are perpetually speaking, the six figures of *The Waves* do not, on the whole, provide much in the way of the sort of ancillary detail or background we have come to expect in a novel.

The point is, clearly, that Virginia Woolf is no longer interested in portraying 'character' in the normal way, but rather in giving the abstract essence of character; as she put it in her diary, 'What I now think (about *The Waves*) is that I can give in a very few strokes the essentials of a person's character', and she adds it should be 'almost as caricature' (9 Apr. 1930). Accordingly the six friends have not characters but *characteristics* which differentiate them from one another, and which hold true throughout the work. Bernard is a 'maker of phrases', endlessly curious about the world and noting it in phrases, Neville embodies rational intelligence and a desire for intellectual precision, Louis suggests a poetic sensitivity wishing to get to the root and concentrate appearances in the crystalline form of some image, Susan, 'glutted with natural happiness', is gifted with a maternal and earthy passion, Jinny, whose 'imagination is the body's', represents the delights of sensual existence, and Rhoda, who 'has no face', no 'weight', the endlessly frustrated desire of dreams. Woolf said that the six were to be 'all different', but the difference remains at the suggestive level of type. The six thus approximate 'humours', another concept from the drama, rather than fully fleshed fictional characters.

Such reduction and concentration with regard to the characters is clearly part of Woolf's attack on 'the novel'. Her desire to get away from the 'fact-recording power' of fiction has led her to write a work which overtly communicates 'very little about the houses, incomes, occupations of its characters'. The speakers are seen in outline rather than in detail, and all the attachments that would bind them to the conventional reality of fiction are held off, suspended as it were, so that they stand further back from life. The purpose of this displacement is clearly to fulfil the aims set forth in 'The Narrow Bridge of Art', allowing Woolf greater flexibility in giving the relation of the mind to general ideas and its soliloquy in solitude. Such concentration is in aid of her more metaphysical intention. Woolf told her husband that the six were meant to examine 'their relation to the fundamental things in human existence', and to facilitate that examination she pares away most of the extraneous and distracting 'detail' which normally occupies fictional characters. The focus of these characters throughout is on the present moment of experience, and they concentrate with a grim intensity on sifting that experience and extracting its fundamental meaning. The book thus has a tremendous reflective and analytical emphasis, as the characters are continually bent over their lives and weighing its significance. Form follows function again: the thickened texture of more material being is removed so that the characters may concentrate on their metaphysical purpose – reality is not allowed to hinder the search for 'the essence of reality'; Woolf strips the characters down to essentials, so as to enable them to get on with the search for essential meaning.

In summary, we can say that the form of *The Waves* undertakes a remarkable *estrangement* of the novel – that is, it pursues a deliberate attempt to de-familiarize or 'make strange' most of the conventional aspects of prose fiction. The illusion of life is determinedly held off through a much greater and more conscious formality. The curiously reduced characters, the static device of their constant, 'poetic' speech, pitches *The Waves* at the level of 'high style' from the beginning, which rapidly distinguishes it from most realistic fiction and achieves a remote and artificial effect. Grasping this general pattern, we are in a position to see clearly where the various impulses and intentions examined in the previous sections were leading – how, that is, her ambitions and aims were translated into practice in *The Waves*. What she has done is to push her art in the direction of a much greater degree of abstraction and stylization, a move which invariably emphasizes artificiality. The effect is not unlike that of classical drama, where similar devices of stylized artifice keep the work elevated and abstract. The difference between this and conventional realism, and even the less conventional realism of Woolf's preceding novels, is acute. An apposite illustration of this difference may be found in Erich Auerbach's classic distinction between the psychological depths and shadows of the Old Testament, 'fraught with background', and the continuous foreground of the Homeric epic, which 'knows only a uniformly illuminated, uniformly objective present'. The calm, relentless narration of the six figures in *The Waves* is similarly calculated to expose or externalize any hidden depths, any secret suggestion, leaving the more usual and mimetic chiaroscuro to fall away. As in *The Odyssey*, nothing remains hidden or unexternalized in *The Waves*; the reader is offered up the most hidden recesses of awareness in a way which distances or displaces the attraction and involvement he experienced with Mrs Dalloway or Lily Briscoe. Clearly Woolf has moved away from the naturalistic effects of her previous work by embracing the abstracting detachment of style.

This is, of course, precisely the direction in which she wanted to move. Her urge to press on with experimentation, to take the novel beyond those 'false' and 'merely conventional' limits, has led her to move in the more overtly artificial direction of poetic drama, away from naturalistic canons of prose fiction toward a more abstract and stylized discourse. Poetry and drama come to the aid of fiction, yielding the 'concentration' she required, a distillation of experience which pared away all prosaic superfluities, and left only essential matter in view. The purpose of this change was to 'concentrate', to bring forward the abstract, the general and the essential. Not realism but 'the essence of reality' was wanted, an aim which meant focusing not on 'detail', or the thickened and distracting texture of real experience, but on its concentrated, reduced and 'essential' aspect. The bizarre and disorienting texture we encounter upon entering *The Waves*, therefore, is the result of the fact that in this work, more so than in any other of Woolf's, the 'modern' principle of form following function was adhered to throughout.

Structure

These various estrangements of form, endeavouring to hold off reality so as to gain a more general and 'essential' perspective, are complemented by the structure of the work. Before we go any further with this analysis, it is as well to make clear how important an aspect of fiction this was to Virginia Woolf. It is ironic that her work persistently has been dismissed as 'precious' or insubstantial, the product of an acute sensibility capable only of a passive registration of the brute press of phenomena, a helpless collapse before the 'incessant shower of innumerable atoms', and possessed of 'no logical power'. Woolf herself protested against the facile view that all she did was 'to float off the contents of [her] mind', observing 'There's a good deal of shaping and composing in my books' (27 Feb. 1926). The fact of the matter is that Woolf's genius was a highly architectonic one, and the *craft* of her fiction is one of its highest achievements. E. M. Forster hit the mark precisely when he described her as 'sensitive, but tough', a remark which echoes the aesthetic capacity she so admired in Proust, namely 'his combination of the utmost sensibility with the utmost tenacity . . . He is tough as catgut and as evanescent as a butterfly's bloom' (8 April 1925). This combination of delicate perception and structural rigour is the idea which animates Lily Briscoe's painting: 'She saw the colour burning on a framework of steel; the light of a butterfly's wing lying upon the arches of a cathedral.' And it is the ideal behind Woolf's own work. For underneath the rapid whirl of sensation and thought, the dizzying stream of mental process which she tries to convey, lies an extremely tightly organized and coherent structure. Out of the apparent randomness and triviality, the chance meetings and stray thoughts of Mrs Dalloway's day in June, for instance, there emerges a pattern of unified concord, made plain at the end when all the stray elements come together at Clarissa's party. In particular the light and dark shades of experience, the bright hostess and obscure demented veteran who have just missed each other throughout the day, come together in a remarkable climax to the novel. *To the Lighthouse* betrays an even more highly organized structure, with its three distinct sections suggesting, as Forster said, a sonata form. The second section, a fast-flowing and lyrical evocation of ten years passing, forms a balancing bridge between the two single days on either side; and again in the final section all the loose threads left hanging in the first part are taken up and resolved in a resonant conclusion. Criticism has not yet begun to do justice to the structural complexity of these works, reinforced as they are by a dense network of interlocking images, phrases, allusions, quotations and other linguistic devices. Not until we begin to approach such works of art on the serious formal level they demand will Woolf's true power and genius be fully appreciated.

The Waves has suffered less from this neglect than have most of her works, simply because, as we might expect in this more artificial and formalized book, the structure is far more apparent. What makes her preceding novels so deceptive, why it is so easy to miss the underlying structural coherence, is precisely her ideal of focusing on the stream of mental perception, and the terrific speed and facility of her verbal prowess. Plunged into the fascinating and absorbing stream of her prose, the reader is swept along as by a rapid current; immersed in the 'luminous halo' of consciousness, we are so impressed by the sense of movement that it is difficult to take bearings or fix upon any structural landmarks. As the goal of producing an illusion of felt life recedes, however, the structure comes to the fore. By slowing down this process, abstracting and distilling experience to external and conscious levels, *The Waves* calls attention to its structural constitution. As Forster put it, 'Here pattern is supreme.' Woolf herself recognized that this work was more highly wrought than its predecessors: 'never, in my life, did I attack such a vague yet elaborate design; whenever I make a mark, I have to think of its relation to a dozen others' (11 Oct. 1929). What this produced was a more abstract and yet visible design.

The structure of *The Waves* has an 'essential' or schematic quality which no reader can miss, since Woolf composed the book out of two starkly contrasting structural elements which alternate throughout the whole work. We have already touched on one of these elements, the soliloquies of the six speakers. These appear in nine distinct sections, each one devoted to a different stage of life. The initial section, the opening of which was quoted above, portrays the six beginning in early childhood noting their surroundings, and the subsequent sections follow the six figures through school, college, early maturity, middle age and, finally, approaching death. In each of these sections, with the important exception of the last, the characters step forward in succession to deliver their speeches, creating a wave-like effect of appearance and withdrawal at an immediate level which recapitulates the larger, rhythmical pattern of the whole. But the main purpose of this structural feature is to expound each age of human life from six different perspectives, thereby creating a mosaic which begins to suggest the contours of a general outline or universal form to human experience.

Pursuing this structural element further, we can begin to clarify the link with Woolf's previous novels. We have seen that the soliloquies give the characters' perceptions of and responses to the present moment of experience, a fact which recapitulates the way Woolf's former works were organized around an intensified apprehension of the present. The opening of *Mrs Dalloway*, for example, focuses on the thoughts of Clarissa's mind as she experiences a particular point in her day – crossing the park on a bright morning. But the difference is that previously Woolf had wished to emphasize the sense of process and duration in experience, and thus had followed the mind over a period of time. Linked with this had been the aim to demonstrate how intensified and highly meaningful 'moments' rise out of the ordinary flow of time as part of the rhythm of common experience – in her terms, to show how 'moments of being' suddenly appear out of the 'grey cotton-wool of existence':

And suddenly the meaning which, for no reason at all, as perhaps they are stepping out of the Tube or ringing a doorbell, descends on people, making them symbolical, making them representative, came upon them, and made them in the dusk standing, looking, the symbols of marriage, husband and wife. Then, after an instant, the symbolical outline which transcended the real figures sank down again, and they became, as they met them, Mr and Mrs Ramsay watching the children throwing catches.

In *The Waves*, however, Woolf wished to 'concentrate', to 'saturate', and so she lifts her characters above the fluid texture of experience. The respective 'moments' are here abstracted from their normal temporal flow and extended throughout the whole of the soliloquy, thus allowing the sense of heightened significance to expand and intensify, giving a deeper and more meditative effect. It is as if she has 'concentrated' those significant moments of previous novels, pared away all else but this, 'the essential thing'. She has now, in effect, 'saturated every atom', and struggled 'to give the moment whole', whatever it includes, with a corresponding gain in depth and weight.

There is, however, another important difference in *The Waves*. The dramatic intensity of her previous work had been achieved by focusing on a short space of time – a day, or part of a day – which was particularly significant and so rich with important and highly charged 'moments' – the day of Clarissa's party when her former lover, Peter Walsh, returns, or the afternoon and early evening of Mrs Ramsay's dinner when the sail to the lighthouse is conceived. But in *The Waves* the structure is once more concentrated and expansive; the 'moments' which the soliloquies bring into focus are now select points drawn from over the entire life-span. Tracing a path through the whole of life by means of these points is obviously a way of standing back from life, tracing the general outline rather than the detail. The thrust is to be comprehensive rather than precise, to explore the larger, more general pattern of human experience over the whole of life rather than to unfold the significance of a particular period. In passing we may note that a similar, comprehensive bent was to operate in her next work, *The Years*, though there the structure expands still further, attempting to incorporate an even more general level of historical transition and change.

The first structural element of the book, the soliloquies, are too prominent to be mistaken or ignored. But these sections of the characters' speech are thrown into relief by the second, markedly contrasting structural feature in the book – the brief, italicized passages which introduce and separate each section of the work. Woolf called these portions 'interludes', and claimed that their function was 'essential; so as to bridge & also give a background ' (26 Jan. 1930). She needed, that is, to provide some medium which would connect the distinct points in time occupied by the characters, one which would also serve as a 'background' throwing the speeches into relief. Certainly it is the contrast to the soliloquies which is most keenly felt in these sections. There is a remote, impersonal aspect in the interludes, which all depict the same elements: a house by the sea, a garden with extremely active birds, the waves breaking on the shore, and, most important, the position of the sun in the sky. Through the use of several devices, the stylized and abstract effect Woolf wished to achieve is intensified through these interludes. Their difference from the soliloquies is emphasized by being printed in italics, and the basic elements depicted herein are rendered in the most highly wrought, rampantly metaphorical style in the book. Most significantly of all, the tone is resolutely 'impersonal'; here a narrative voice does emerge, but it is not one which can be located, identified or placed.

The sun had not yet risen. The sea was indistinguishable from the sky, except that the sea was slightly creased as if a cloth had wrinkles in it. Gradually as the sky whitened a dark line lay on the horizon dividing the sea from the sky and the grey cloth became barred with thick strokes moving, one after another, beneath the surface, following each other, pursuing each other, perpetually.

As they neared the shore each bar rose, heaped itself, broke and swept a thin veil of white water across the sand. The wave paused, and then drew out again, sighing like a sleeper whose breath comes and goes unconsciously. Gradually the dark bar on the horizon became clear as if the sediment in an old wine-bottle has sunk and left the glass green. Behind it, too, the sky cleared as if the white sediment there had sunk, or as if the arm of a woman couched beneath the horizon had raised a lamp and flat bars of white, green and yellow spread across the sky like the blades of a fan. Then she raised her lamp higher and the air seemed to become fibrous and to tear away from the green surface flickering and flaming in red and yellow fibres like the smoky fire that roars from a bonfire. Gradually the fibres of the burning bonfire were fused into one haze, one incandescence which lifted the weight of the woollen grey sky on top of it and turned it to a million atoms of soft blue. The surface of the sea slowly became transparent and lay rippling and sparkling until the dark stripes were almost rubbed out. Slowly the arm that held the lamp raised it higher and then higher until a broad flame became visible; an arc of fire burnt on the rim of the horizon, and all round it the sea blazed gold.

The light struck upon the trees in the garden, making one leaf transparent and then another. One bird chirped high up; there was a pause; another chirped lower down. The sun sharpened the walls of the house, and rested like the tip of a fan upon a white blind and made a blue finger-print of shadow under the leaf by the bedroom window. The blind stirred slightly, but all was dim and unsubstantial. The birds sang their blank melody outside.

Attentive readers of Virginia Woolf may recall having come across a similar piece of writing before: it is that 'bridging' section of *To the Lighthouse*, where the personal focus drops away and a lyrical and impersonal one rises to take over. Woolf once said that *The Waves* was to be an 'abstract, mystical, eyeless book', a description which closely echoed her original intentions for the middle section of *To the Lighthouse*: 'here is the most difficult abstract piece of writing – I have to give an empty house, no people's characters, the passage of time, all eyeless & featureless with nothing to cling to' (30 Apr. 1926). By the strange term 'eyeless' she clearly meant impersonal, 'no people's characters' to cling to as opposed to her usual 'method' of filtering narrative through a character's consciousness. And indeed the 'interludes' in *The Waves* sometimes approximate quite closely this second section of *To the Lighthouse*:

But what after all is one night? A short space, especially when the darkness dims so soon, and so soon a bird sings, a cock crows, or a faint green quickens, like a turning leaf, in the hollow of the wave. Night, however, succeeds to night. The winter holds a pack of them in store and deals them equally, evenly, with indefatigable fingers. They lengthen; they darken. Some of them hold aloft clear planets, plates of brightness. The autumn trees, ravaged as they are, take on the flash of tattered flags kindling in the gloom of cool cathedral caves where gold letters on marble pages describe death in battle and how bones bleach and burn far away in Indian sands. The autumn trees gleam in the yellow moonlight, in the light of harvest moons, the light which mellows the energy of labour, and smoothes the stubble, and brings the wave lapping blue to the shore.

There is a marked similarity of style here, with parallels in rhythm and diction, along with many recurrent features of imagery – e.g. the effects of light and darkness on an interior, the natural surroundings of a house by the sea. Such parallels begin to suggest the strong link between the two pieces of writing. Moreover, the title of the section of *To the Lighthouse* is 'Time Passes', which is the import of the interludes in *The Waves*. Each interlude shows the sun in a different position in the sky, so that taken together they depict the passage of a single day, which measures out the advancing life of the characters. What Woolf has done, in effect, is to invert the previous structural device: to stretch the central, bridging section of the earlier work into a containing

frame in the latter; a swift passage of ten years which joins
the two days on either side has been transformed into a single
day which encloses and frames the whole life-span of the six
characters.

It is the relation and interplay of these contrasted structures
which give *The Waves* much of its thematic interest. Here we
may simply observe that by interspersing these 'impersonal'
sections amongst the soliloquies, Woolf further reinforces the
'wave' pattern of the book; the intermittence of description
and reflection forms a progressive rise and fall, the
withdrawal or ebb of personality occurring after each surge
of speech has been spent. The contrast achieved here is very
much to the point. Woolf noted that the 'background' she
meant to give to the characters was 'the sea; insensitive
nature', and clearly one function of the interludes was to
suggest the natural world *outside* the confines of human
thought. The 'background' to the human speech is 'what we
are not', her attempt to convey 'what exists when we are not
there'. By means of the controlling structure alone, then, the
sensitive and the insensitive, the personal and the impersonal,
consciousness and phenomena are thrown into continual
effective counterpoint. Such concentrated effects of structure
heighten the sense of the book as abstract art, and prepare the
way for the more expansive engagements of the book's
principal theme, to which we must now turn.

Chapter 4

Theme

The power of process

At one point, while deep in the struggle to compose *The Waves*, Woolf suggested that the work had 'a large & potential theme', which *Orlando* had lacked (28 Mar. 1930). This comment remains curiously close to the mark, even without a knowledge of her intentions. Every reader, however baffled or confused, must sense the presence of some large and meaningful ambition behind the strangeness of the work. Yet discovering precisely what that 'theme' is is not an easy task, since it tends to remain in the realm of 'potential' rather than emerging with any distinctness and clarity. This is partly due to the abstracting elements of the form; but it is also owing to the fact, as I indicated at the outset, that the book is replete with meaning — it is, in the current phrase, 'overdetermined'. The highly conscious intelligence of the speakers presents the *point* of each perception the moment it is grasped, and this is multiplied in the book to the extent that an overall 'meaning' is obscured. We get a profusion of reports, a surfeit of eloquent comment at each stage from six different perspectives, with the result that there is a plethora of perceptions, implications and understandings, a multiplication of 'potential' meanings, which is confusing, contradictory and destructive of coherence. For all the abstract and strongly marked features of structure and form, our experience of reading *The Waves* is one of continuous metamorphosis and transformation — very like the waves, in fact. To adopt a musical analogy, there are so many variations going on that the 'theme' all but vanishes.

This fluidity of texture is itself part of the thematic purpose of the work. We remarked briefly on this effect at the beginning of the study, commenting on the way in which *The Waves* absorbs its readers and disorients the critical faculties. Thus far, however, the analysis has been considerably simplified, ignoring the welter of the waves for the sake of critical clarity. We have followed the lead of Woolf's given intentions and pursued a policy of abstraction in dealing with the book – that is to say, we have emphasized the work's static, stylized and abstract effect, in line with her high ambitions of moving away from the novel. To come to grips with the *theme*, however, means a reversal of this procedure, bringing into account this other, equally important aspect of the book thus far excluded. We may recall Woolf's being haunted by the contradiction as to whether life was 'very solid or very shifting', and *The Waves* explores both sides of the contradiction. The fact that this aspect goes against the grain of what we have observed thus far increases the complexity of the work, and heightens its paradoxical nature; but it also accounts for its dominant thematic interest.

Hitherto, we have emphasized the abstracting power of form, pointing out the way certain formal and structural aspects of *The Waves* seek to detach the characters from life, and hold off the usual sense of novelistic reality. Form, however, is the pressure of intention meeting the resistance of materials, a dialectical process which synthesizes something different than what first rose in the mind. Just as Woolf's obscure 'impulse' went through a number of drastic alterations, so her thematic intentions were subject to transformation. The fact is that for all its static and condensing drive *The Waves* retains a strong sense of movement, change, development – precisely that sense of 'life' which the formal structure attempts to remove. This occurs on many levels, from the sophisticated linguistic rhythms, constantly urging the work forward, to the elemental fact that the characters progress from youth to age. Paradoxical as it may seem, *The Waves* embodies an element of *process*, which is antithetical to the abstracting function of its *form*.

This duality offers an endlessly alternating series of critical perspectives on the work, a wave-like overlapping which holds much of the book's interest. And it was central to the work from the beginning. We may recall here that at that point of origin Woolf's notion of 'the essence of reality' was linked to that 'oddest affair' of life − a latent duality she was to unfold while developing her thoughts about *The Moths*: 'They might be islands of light − islands in the stream that I am trying to convey: life itself going on' (28 May 1929). 'They' (the moths) were soon to go, but in a sense the two contrasting features outlined here remained: it is not difficult to see those suspended and intensified soliloquies on the present moment representing those 'islands of light', while the characters' cumulative development, their collective and progressive experience through the work renders that 'stream' of 'life itself'. The static isolation and absorbing process are opposed elements at the root of the work.

To perceive properly the thematic movement of *The Waves* is to grasp the counterthrust of life against form. We must not exaggerate this conflict, since 'life itself' is subjected to an abstracting stress in the book, not given in the 'appalling business' of a mechanical progression from lunch to dinner, but rather in a sequence of select points over the whole course, the 'essence' of life. Yet for all its formal remoteness, *The Waves* retains a link with life − which is as much to say that abstraction does not dispel verisimilitude; if anything it enhances or 'concentrates' it. We said the characters here are held off or suspended from direct participation in reality, but this is actually so they may better register their awareness of life. Woolf has lifted her human figures out of that 'stream' onto 'islands of light', but this serves only to concentrate their focus on the procession. Hence, paradoxically, through all the detaching and condensing artifice of the work, the sextet's *experience* of 'life itself' comes to the fore. Here, of course, the mimetic and naturalistic elements are smuggled back into the book, since under cover of an 'abstract' disguise, Woolf is trying to give some sense of what 'life' is like − 'the stream that I am trying to convey'. And as we might expect, 'the novel' re-enters the work here as well. The subject of change and growth and development is the subject of most works of fiction, and process is the foundation of narrative. Try as she might to banish 'the novel' from this work, it remains imbued in the form; similarly, for all that the form seeks to withhold 'life', that 'stream' contrives to enter and 'saturate' the work. Herein lies a deep tension between art and life, abstraction and empathy which is at the heart of *The Waves*, and which springs from her paradoxical wish to 'eliminate' yet 'put everything in'. This tension is the main subject of the following chapter, and here we need only to acknowledge the counterbalancing devotion to process and change which opens the way to the book's theme.

The contrast or tension between these two elements soon becomes prominent in *The Waves*. We have seen that the characters' attention is fixed on their experience or awareness of life, and it quickly becomes clear that one of the primary components of that awareness is precisely this sense of 'process'; the 'essential' experience of life seems to be one of change, flux, a rapid 'stream': Bernard observes, 'Everybody seems to be doing things for this moment only; and never again. Never again. The urgency of it all is fearful'; and Louis says, 'I am conscious of the flux, of disorder, of annihilation and despair.' The six may be suspended from that stream while they speak, but they do not escape it — they are not in it, but they are of it. Indeed their vantage point of heightened awareness seems to 'concentrate' the general sense of time passing, and intensify their perception of its effects:

'And time', said Bernard, 'lets fall its drop. The drop that has formed on the roof of the soul falls. On the roof of my mind time, forming, lets fall its drop. Last week, as I stood shaving, the drop fell. I, standing with my razor in my hand, became suddenly aware of the merely habitual nature of my action . . . All through the day's work, at intervals, my mind went to an empty place, saying, "What is lost? What is over?" and "Over and done with", I muttered, "over and done with", solacing myself with words. People noticed the vacuity of my face and the aimlessness of my conversation. The last words of my sentence tailed away. And as I buttoned on my coat to go home I said more dramatically, "I have lost my youth." '

The interplay between the two structural elements of the book is vital in reinforcing this theme. It soon becomes clear that the initial item in each of the interludes, the position of the sun in the sky, corresponds to the age of the speakers. The dawn depicted in the opening of the book (quoted above, p. 55) sets the scene for their infancy, while subsequent stages of their progress along life's way are marked by such opening phrases as: 'The sun rose', 'The sun had risen to its full height', 'The sun was sinking', and so on. 'Our brief day in the sun' is of course a standard poetic conceit, and here the notion serves as an animating structural device: the growth and ageing of the six being imaged in the progress of the sun. What this does is to frame the activities and experience of the characters clearly within the passage of time, and as we might expect the feeling produced by this device changes as the book progresses. In the first half of the book, their bright morning of existence as it were, the world is charged with a sense of discovery and wonder, of testing and exploring possibilities in life. Their youth grants them, for the most part, an ease and authority in existence, and here the sun seems to be in league with the characters. In the second half, however, 'time that gave doth now his gift confound'; as the sun starts to descend, there is an increasing sense of anxiety and conflict developed between the two realms. The acute consciousness of the speakers becomes progressively burdened by mortality; the lengthening shadows thrown by the sinking sun press with increasing weight on the soliloquies as they measure their dwindling stock of time. 'We are doomed, all of us' exclaims Neville, though it is Bernard who shows most awareness of 'our eternal flux': 'How swift life runs from January to December! We are all swept by on the torrent of things.'

It is common to note how such sentiments echo those of their creator, and it will be useful to bring out the parallel with Woolf's own position. If we read through her diaries of this period we see at once that such reflections were very much on *her* mind: 'And death – as I always feel – hurrying near. 43: how many more books?' (7 Dec. 1925), she wrote after the completion of *Mrs Dalloway*. And after *To the Lighthouse* had been published she was again gripped by 'This insatiable desire to write something before I die, this ravaging sense of the shortness & feverishness of life' (20 Dec. 1927). Similarly after she had begun *The Waves* she observed, 'I am impressed by the transitoriness of human life to such an extent that I am often saying a farewell' (28 Mar. 1929). Clearly Woolf has transmitted much of her own position on 'life' to *The Waves*, a point to which we will return. Yet this is only an amplification of themes sounded in Woolf's previous novels. The different positions of the sun in the interludes here fulfil much the same function as the periodic tolling of Big Ben in *Mrs Dalloway* − a work which, significantly enough, was originally entitled *The Hours*. And the waves themselves, which contribute to this thematic pressure through the contrast of their eternal recurrence with the finite lives of the characters, had appeared in a similar guise in *To the Lighthouse*. At one point Mrs Ramsay was found listening to

the monotonous fall of the waves on the beach, which for the most part beat a measured and soothing tatoo to her thoughts and seemed consolingly to repeat over and over again as she sat with the children the words of some old cradle song, murmured by nature . . . but at other times suddenly and unexpectedly . . . had no such kindly meaning, but like a ghostly roll of drums remorselessly beat the measure of life, made one think of the destruction of the island and its engulfment in the sea, and warned her whose day had slipped past in one quick doing after another that it was all ephemeral as a rainbow . . .

Clearly the theme of time and its implied sense of dissolution and flux had long been a focal concern of Virginia Woolf's, and it forms a particularly palpable element in *The Waves* due to the structural features which reinforce and call attention to it. Here perhaps we can see why Woolf has often been linked with Walter Pater. It is evident that a sensibility which refines its focus on the mental flux of sensations will be all too apt to develop a heightened awareness of the end of that flux − intensifying consciousness will make one all too mindful of its cessation. Pater gave particularly eloquent expression to this late Romantic position, especially in the famous 'Conclusion' to *The Renaissance*. Consciously assuming the mantle of Heraclitus ('nothing remains'), Pater's evocation of the 'rapid whirlpool' of consciousness, 'a drift of momentary arts of sight and passion and thought', was similarly haunted by transience. His writing is charged with a 'sense of the splendour of our experience and of its awful brevity' and 'gathering all we are into one desperate effort to see and touch'. These sentences seem to register exactly the anxious and urgent sensibilities of the characters in *The Waves*.

What is most significant, however, is the response this awareness of time and flux generates. Pater's weary tone always implies a resignation, a cultivation of the 'highest moments as they pass', but a more or less passive acceptance of the situation. Such an attitude is not true of the characters in *The Waves*: 'To let oneself be carried on passively is unthinkable', says Bernard, and the work abounds with images of battle or combat. 'Oppose ourselves to this illimitable chaos . . . this formless imbecility', says Neville; the perception of their predicament rouses these characters to act and to mount a challenge on the 'stream' of time which takes them toward death. At one point Woolf herself revealed the theme of the work was that 'effort, effort, dominates: not the waves: & personality: & defiance' (22 Dec. 1930). Here she outlines the essential thematic conflict of the book: consciousness must struggle to 'resist' the blank world of phenomena, the personal must 'oppose' the impersonal, the human voice must challenge the inhuman monotony of the waves. Speaking for the group, Bernard declares himself aware of 'the presence of those enemies who change, but are always there; the forces we fight against'. Those changeful 'enemies' of consciousness include time, dissolution, the inchoate existence of nature, and death − all represented in the interludes, which are 'always there' in the book. This perception drives the characters to 'fight, fight' as Bernard says throughout, to struggle against these inimical forces − a struggle which progressively emerges as the work's central theme.

Resisting the flood

The larger thematic pattern of *The Waves* is now coming clear. The six characters are meant on the one hand to experience that 'stream' of 'life itself', and to register the experience of that process fully. For this purpose, they are distanced from a complete immersion in the 'stream' to which they are necessarily bound, and this allows the reflective and thoughtful element in the book to deepen. They seek out, as it were, 'the essence of reality', but increasingly that 'essence' takes on a negative cast, a tapering, dwindling enclosure. Thus their account of 'life' turns into a rigorous search of appearance, to find something which can 'resist' the flood. We recall Woolf's own 'restless search' for 'it', some satisfying, metaphysical discovery within 'life itself' which resolves one's anxieties about transience and ageing; these six characters become anxious questors in the same vein.

What then, are the means of resistance? What are the resources which help human consciousness to 'oppose' this flood? One of the principal means explored in *The Waves* is friendship. Earlier we observed the fact that the sort of human relationships we normally expect to find in a novel — those involving wives, husbands, children, lovers — in this work become peripheral and ancillary. This is chiefly because the book brings the relation of the six friends themselves to the fore — undoubtedly part of Woolf's tribute to the one group within her life, which became so central and important, Bloomsbury. At one point, after completing *Mrs Dalloway*, she wrote that 'if 6 people died, it is true that my life would cease: by wh[ich] I mean, it would run so thin that though it might go on, would it have any relish?' (27 Nov. 1925). This sense of crucial, central friendships within a group is a great part of the effect of *The Waves*. While it is true that they are not always occupied in their relations with each other (thankfully the book cannot be read as a transcription of Bloomsbury's letters), the awareness of the others is never far away from the consciousness of any speaker; and the fact of the group is the one stable centre to which they invariably return. Indeed, their relation to each other, the animating awareness of themselves *as* a group, resolves into a wave-like movement of its own, a constant pattern of breaking and re-grouping, of unity and dispersion throughout the book.

We see the thematic impact of this movement most clearly at those occasions when the sense of unity is at its height. There are two such occasions in *The Waves*, in the fourth and eighth sections respectively; and here *The Waves* follows the pattern laid down by earlier novels, namely enacting a movement towards a climactic 'moment of being' in the communal gathering of a party. Clarissa Dalloway's party and Mrs Ramsay's dinner are the immediate forebears of these scenes in *The Waves*, where the six friends meet for dinner − literally a communion − in restaurants. The driving impulse in each case is to engender a moment of community which seeks to oppose the destructive stream of time. Thus two scenes recapitulate that of Mrs Ramsay's triumphant dinner in *To the Lighthouse*, where the guests were suddenly united and 'were all conscious of making a party together in a hollow, on an island; had their common cause against that fluidity out there'. The 'fluidity' outside in this case was the sea, whose destructive and dissolvent effect appeared throughout the work; but the figures in *The Waves* face the same 'enemy', albeit more symbolically imaged.

The first of these scenes occurs in the fourth 'episode', where the six friends gather at a London restaurant to bid farewell to their common friend, Percival, who is off to India. This section represents the climax of their morning of experience, a point when the 'crown' of maturity sits easily and happily upon them. 'How proudly we sit here', said Jinny, 'we who are not yet twenty-five! . . . Emerged from the tentative ways, the obscurities and dazzle of youth, we look straight in front of us, ready for what may come.' Most of the section is taken up with a lengthy review of those 'tentative ways' they have explored in the past three sections, leaving them with a clarified understanding of their life so far. This in turn leads to that extraordinary 'moment' wherein they come together in an intense unity, experiencing a 'poetic' transport, which seems to lift them out of time.

'Now once more,' said Louis, 'as we are about to part, having paid our bill, the circle in our blood, broken so often, so sharply, for we are so different, closes in a ring. Something is made. Yes, as we rise and fidget, a little nervously, we pray, holding in our hands this common feeling, "Do not move, do not let the swing door cut to pieces the thing that we have made, that globes itself here, among these lights, these peelings, this litter of bread crumbs and people passing. Do not move, do not go. Hold it for ever." '

'Let us hold it for one moment,' said Jinny; 'love, hatred, by whatever name we call it, this globe whose walls are made of Percival, of youth and beauty, and something so deep sunk within us that we shall perhaps never make this moment out of one man again.'

'Forests and far countries on the other side of the world,' said Rhoda, 'are in it; seas and jungles; the howlings of jackals and moonlight falling upon some high peak where the eagle soars.'

'Happiness is in it,' said Neville, 'and the quiet of ordinary things. A table, a chair, a book with a paper-knife stuck between the pages . . .'

'Week-days are in it,' said Susan, 'Monday, Tuesday, Wednesday; the horses going up to the fields and the horses returning; the rooks rising and falling, and catching the elm-trees in their net, whether it is April, whether it is November.'

'What is to come is in it,' said Bernard. 'That is the last drop and the brightest that we let fall like some supernal quicksilver into the swelling and splendid moment created by us from Percival . . . We have proved, sitting eating, sitting talking, that we can add to the treasury of moments. We are not slaves bound to suffer incessantly unrecorded petty blows on our bent backs . . . We are creators. We too have made something that will join the innumerable congregations of past time.'

The image of the globe, which is so prominent here, had a special resonance for Woolf — indeed this entire passage seems to have been derived from another diary entry:

So the days pass & I ask myself sometimes whether one is not hypnotised, as a child by a silver globe, by life; & whether this is living. Its very quick, bright, exciting. But superficial perhaps. I should like to take the globe in my hands & feel it quietly, round, smooth, heavy, & so hold it, day after day.   (28 Nov. 1928)

Here in *The Waves*, the six speakers appear to have achieved this desire, as they put life into a globe — distilling and concentrating its 'essence' — and so 'hold it' among them for a moment. To borrow another phrase, the six 'restless searchers' seem at last to have found 'it', to have reached a point where 'the thing in itself is enough, satisfactory; achieved'. They have pooled their experience and mutually created a 'moment' of understanding and significance which defeats the usual enemies of dissolution and flux. It is clear that this 'moment of being' they enjoy lifts them temporarily out of the reach of time, a 'triumph', which may remind us of another such 'moment' in Woolf's work. At the climax of Mrs Ramsay's dinner she discovers 'all round them' a similar 'moment' which 'partook . . . of eternity; . . . there is a coherence in things, a stability; something, she meant, is immune from change, and shines out . . . in the face of the flowing, the fleeting, the spectral, like a ruby . . . Of such moments, she thought, the thing is made that remains for ever after. This would remain.'

There is, of course, a further similarity in that both 'moments of being' are so thoroughly hedged round by their momentariness; the transcendent experience is only temporary. With her foot on the threshhold as she goes out of the room, Mrs Ramsay feels that her 'moment' had 'become already the past'. Similarly here in *The Waves*, the 'effort' of keeping the globe aloft, out of the reach of time, is spurred by the sense that the moment will pass, drop back into 'the flowing, the fleeting' current of time. Even so, in both cases 'the thing in itself is enough', the achievement of having 'made' such a moment fortifies the creators, giving them the sense that they are not merely the subjugated slaves of time but 'can add to the treasury of moments'. This clearly is an experience which fortifies their engagement with life.

One of the most interesting features of this long hymn to the moment is its absolute dependence on Percival. Percival is such a crucial figure in the book that a brief digression in order to give an account of his structural and thematic purpose is necessary. He emerges in the second section, while the six are at school, and as a character is nearly a caricature of the Public School 'blood' – manly but sensitive, a superb sportsman, and an unquestioned leader of men. 'His magnificence is that of some medieval commander', according to Louis, and all of the six are, in some way or another, 'in love' with Percival. The most telling thing about him, however, is that in a book suffused with soliloquy he never speaks; he is not on the hyperconscious plane which the others inhabit, but rather represents an unconscious ease and naturalness of existence, a perfect accommodation with reality, which the others all long for but can never reach. 'He sees nothing; he hears nothing. He is remote from us all in a pagan universe', says Neville, rather accurately describing the gulf that exists between them. He is, if you like, a figure of 'life itself', a representative of mere being, and as such the meeting point between the world of the interludes and that of the soliloquies, a balance between sensitive and 'insensitive nature': 'Not a thread, not a sheet of paper lies between him and the sun', as Neville says. Percival thus suggests the possibility of perfect human acclimatization in the world, undivided by the incessant self-consciousness of the others. This, of course, is precisely his attraction for them, since he seems to contain the secret of human life in the world which they are all trying discover.

At any rate, Percival, and the sense of youth and beauty he represents, draws them together here at his parting, serving as a focus for the intense, heightened 'moment of being' they create. Significantly, however, it is a farewell dinner, and the farewells they bid become a permanent part of their experience. For the next section opens with the stark words: 'He is dead.' Percival is doomed to an absurd death in India, falling off his horse as it stumbles, and his death is their first real experience of the 'enemy', one which destroys the sense of youth, and endless possibility which had been enshrined before. Percival's death inaugurates the second half of their day, the declining sun, and after this 'satiety and doom; the sense of what is unescapable in our lot; death; the knowledge of limitations; how life is more obdurate than one had thought it' never leave them. In particular the binding power which drew them together disappears, and the six become progressively fragmented, sealed in the encroachments of established identity, middle age, and personal endeavour. Custom hangs upon them with a weight heavy as frost and deep almost as life. They scarcely see one another in the time covered by the three sections after Percival's death, and attempt, on the whole, to ignore time through busy activity, rather than trying actively to resist it.

Yet the book does bring about one further union of the six in the eighth section of the work, where they meet at Hampton Court. This is a highly structured parallel to their first union in the fourth section, but it serves rather as a parody of that occasion – both because they are now enmeshed in identities which they do not really wish to give up, and because Percival's absence is as palpably felt among them now as his presence had been before. In this *The Waves* is closely following the thematic progression of *To the Lighthouse*, as in the third section of that work the remnants of the first group meet again without Mrs Ramsay present, and her absence casts a similar dark cloud over the attempt. The six figures in *The Waves* do reach another 'moment' of shared knowledge, but darkly now, with a more negative weight. As Bernard sums it up, 'We saw for a moment laid out among as the body of the complete human being whom we have failed to be, but at the same time, cannot forget.' That body is both the dead body of Percival, and the fallen 'body' of their own communal feeling, a dramatic contrast to the high unity they experienced before. Moreover, the sense of those 'limitations' is now overwhelming; as they approach their own 'night', the sense of time about them is unmistakable. Thus, when the six *do* join together at the end of the meal, it is not in a metaphysical 'ring', creating a bright globe of life, but it is hand in hand walking six abreast into the darkness, a phalanx attacking time and the night which is suffused by a fearful, urgent and defensive quality.

Bernard's summing up

To end the work at this point would have been a pessimistic and dispiriting conclusion; the six characters' exploration of life would seem to lead to a steady dwindling of possibility, a loss in the struggle against time and the waves. However, the book does not end here; there is one further effort of 'defiance', which becomes the most extended and significant of all. This is the last section of speech, the final assertion of 'personality' which is given entirely to Bernard. It was in fact of this section Woolf wrote her comment about making the theme 'effort, effort' dominate over the waves, and it gives an entirely new cast to the work. Previously, as we have seen, the six characters have been engaged in intensely scrutinizing their lives at particular points in its progress, and commenting one after the other on the moment. Here, however, 'this affair of being is done', the urgency drops away, and a single meditative voice is heard throughout a section which is longer than any other by a good way. The rhythm as it were slows and deepens, to a reflective, contemplative cast. For here Bernard looks back over his life; he is, in effect, recapitulating that ambition which sparked the book itself, namely to 'stand further back from life', to get hold of its larger contours and take the measure of its general pattern. To emphasize this shift, the stylistic conventions previously adopted fall away; Woolf provides him with a silent auditor in a restaurant so that he is not soliloquizing in a void, and the pure present tense drops back into a more normal narrative past. What he is trying to do now is not to report on experience as it takes place, but 'to sum up', to give the 'whole' of his life, by which he really means its final form. It is an impossible undertaking to give the whole of life, an impossibility he freely and continually admits; but he is actually trying, with varying success, to 'concentrate' and extract his life's 'essence', to distill the 'one true story' out of the confusing and chaotic manifold of experience. He often seems, as we read, to be giving that confusion and chaos more than its due, but the 'effort' to come to some clarified understanding and give form and shape to the formless content of his life persists. Thus his opening statement: 'The illusion is on me that something adheres for a moment, has roundness, weight, depth, is completed. This, for the moment, seems to be my life.'

We recognize at once the echoes of the previous 'moment of being' in the fourth chapter, taking up the 'globe' of life and 'holding it' close 'for a moment'. Thus at the outset of this final speech we are given notice of a similar undertaking, though this time is will occur in a far more relaxed, patient, unfolding way than the urgent achievement before. (Here indeed Woolf seems to be surreptitiously enacting the ideal expressed in her diary entry of 28 Nov. 1928: 'to take the globe in my hands & feel it quietly, round, smooth, heavy . . .'.) The same sense of coherent grasp and undertanding of life is signalled, leading us to expect another occasion of resistance to the 'enemy' of dissolution and flux. Moreover, as before, the globe is a communal one: 'this globe is full of figures', Bernard says, reflecting the fact that, as we have seen, his experience of life has been inextricably bound up with those of his friends: 'I do not altogether know who I am – Jinny, Susan, Neville, Rhoda or Louis; or how to distinguish my life from theirs.' To get to the clarified 'essence' of his life, then, Bernard must sift theirs along with it. Thus, in this final movement of the work, Bernard effectively 'tells the story' of what we have just read, recounting the events of the eight preceding sections. We may recall here that in the early stages of thinking about this work, Woolf envisaged 'some semi-mystic very profound life', which would 'all be told on one occasion'; this final section is evidently the remnant of that vague original conception. At any rate, the change this introduces into the work is considerable; the events and activities of the six characters, whose confusing multiplicity we have just experienced, are now seen again from a single perspective, with a considerable gain in coherence. It is no accident that many of the distinct, crystallized phrases which I, along with most critics, employ to explain the occurrences earlier in the work come from this final section. By introducing it, Woolf places a clarifying and focusing lens over the events of past experience, and this contributes enormously to the sense of 'roundness, weight, depth', and completion.

The theme of the book (we have said before) tends to stand out most clearly at those moments of 'unity' when the six friends come together. And so it is here, but with the difference of a totally new emphasis. For this integration occurs in the mind of Bernard; the last communal event, and last effort of defeating the wasting process of life, belongs to the imagination. The 'globe' we remember was seen as a 'creation', and 'telling the story' is an imaginative art, inseparable from the imaginative procedures of ordering and shaping. The final resource against the ravaging time turns out to be the human mind itself, its 'shaping spirit of imagination', capable of ordering and shaping life into art. This is of course the resource that Woolf herself relied on most. Here is another parallel with *To the Lighthouse*, for the final effort in that work was Lily's painting, an imaginative effort which similarly mirrored the creation of the 'moment of being' before. Bernard qualifies his effort by the term 'illusion', indicating how provisional and contingent is the ordering, and showing an awareness of how much such an artificial and abstracting element distorts the actual experience of 'life itself'. Nevertheless, he persists in his effort and provides the one satisfying attempt at reaching a coherence.

This implies that art is the ultimate and most significant resistance to the shapelessness of life; the ordering imagination is given the last word. This had been true for much of Woolf's work, and indeed the theme had been sounded periodically throughout *The Waves* itself. Louis exhibits throughout the poet's urge for order: 'If I do not nail these impressions to the board and out of the many men in me make one . . . then I shall fall like snow and be wasted', and he carries on this struggle in the 'attic room' of poetry. More telling is Rhoda's experience of a concert upon hearing of Percival's death; she listen to a string quartet by Beethoven and reaches the following solace:

'Like' and 'like' and 'like' — but what is the thing that lies beneath the semblance of the thing? Now that lightning has gashed the tree and the flowering branch has fallen and Percival, by his death, has made me this gift, let me see the thing. There is a square; there is an oblong. The players take that square and place it upon the oblong. They place it very accurately; they make a perfect dwelling place. Very little is left outside. The structure is now visible; what is inchoate is here stated; we are not so various or so mean; we have made oblongs and stood them upon squares. This is our triumph; this is our consolation.

Significantly, it is neither of these two 'visionaries' and solitaries who is given the final task of summing up, but rather Bernard, the putative novelist. This must be seen as Woolf's tribute to her own art, which was capable, she constantly hoped, of encompassing both 'vision' and 'fact'. Bernard's interest in the world, his curiosity about life, makes him a more fitting spokesman for the six, a more appropriate questor for the 'essence of reality'. Thus he makes the final effort to join the many men into one, and to state the inchoate and make the structure visible.

Myth and the self

Bernard's imaginative absorption of his six companions suggests another, extremely intriguing aspect to the thematic dimension of *The Waves*. Woolf herself told her husband while writing the book that she 'wanted to take six persons, intimate friends, all different, and show their relations to the fundamental things in human existence', a remark suggesting her desire to 'abstract' and portray the 'essential' aspect of life. However, Leonard went on to report: 'At the same time . . . she wanted to show that these six persons were severally facets of a single complete person.' This extraordinary ambition was confirmed in a letter she wrote to G. L. Dickinson soon after *The Waves* was published, where she remarked, 'the six characters were supposed to be one'. The problem of the one and the many has long been a standard issue in philosophy, so perhaps we should not be wholly surprised to find it occurring in this most 'philosophical' of her books. All the same, it is difficult to know quite how to interpret this cryptic suggestion within the context of the book itself.

One possibility is that Woolf is referring to the *group* or corporate body which the six friends compose. We have seen

how friendship is an important theme in the work, and there
are numerous indications that their experience is communal
rather than individual. We recall that the relationships which
came into focus here are really only those among the six, and
this exclusivity is maintained by their habit of constantly
referring to one another – 'I do not want, as Jinny wants,
to be admired' (Susan); 'My scope embraces what Neville
never reaches' (Bernard). As Bernard accurately puts it: 'We
use our friends to measure our own stature.' Furthermore,
there is a continual process of comment or reflection upon
how one or more of the others would react to this or that
sight, incident or event – for example Rhoda's perceptive
summary of how each of the other five will respond to the
news of Percival's death in the fifth section. All of this keeps
the group dynamics and experience to the forefront of the
work, suggesting that each individual life is part of the larger
entity of the group. It is this which seems to be in Bernard's
mind when he comes to look back over his life in the work's
final soliloquy: 'I am not one person; I am many people; I do
not altogether know who I am – Jinny, Susan, Neville,
Rhoda or Louis; or how to distinguish my life from theirs.'

There is, however, another level of implication at work
here, something at once more 'mystical' and 'essential' than
group dynamics. A clue to this appears in the draft manuscript, where Woolf indicated that the title of the work
might be 'the life of anyone'. We recall that Woolf's intention in approaching this book was to convey the larger,
more general perspectives of experience, giving the universal
outline of 'life itself'. To this end she has restricted her
characterization, attempting to keep it to some extent at the
level of type. Her six characters are thus representative –
rational intelligence, sensual instinct, maternal passion, and
so on; and in this light their joint experience would suggest a
comprehensive account of possibilities and perspectives in
human life. Taken in a cradle-to-grave survey, their collective
experience thereby gestures towards the largest and most
general outline of all, the universal dimension of myth; the
'single complete person' they were meant to suggest would in

this sense be that 'life of anyone' or the universal experience of humanity itself.

In this light the particular fictional account of the six lives was meant to suggest the universal experience of human life itself, and the sum of their experience to point to a mythic meaning at the highest level of generality. Such a symbolic resonance is, of course, a familiar and time-honoured feature of poetry, from the medieval Everyman, being both an individual and all men, to Pope's Windsor Forest, representing both a particular place and all pastoral pleasure. Such a symbolic dimension, however, has been difficult to sustain in the local habitation of prose fiction, with its penchant for individual character, precise contexts and particular detail. Even Leopold Bloom in Joyce's *Ulysses* has more to do with the gritty facts of petty bourgeois life in Dublin than the ancient king he is meant to invoke. Yet this sort of trafficking between the specific and general meaning was clearly one of the features of 'poetry' Woolf wished to appropriate for that fiction of the future she described in 'The Narrow Bridge of Art'; and she has done her best, by paring away the novelistic features to their 'essential' outlines, to inculcate this in *The Waves*. To break with the conventional mimetic thrust of the novel and 'saturate' the work with poetry meant to establish a resonance between the fictional particular and poetic universal; the busy, anxious reflections of her six protagonists as they experience 'life' are meant collectively to suggest the more general outline of human life itself. Perhaps the closest analogue to this kind of mythic manipulation occurs in the poems of William Blake, whose 'giant forms' are at once distinct beings (each with a particular temperament and type) and component parts of a single complete being. Blake called this larger being Albion, a mythic representation of Mankind itself, and Woolf's effort moves in the same direction.

One sees this dimension of the work most clearly in those communal scenes where the sense of unity is at a height. At such points the borders of individual identity begin to waver and fade out and their larger, symbolic outline begins to appear. At Percival's farewell dinner, Bernard captures this sense in a marvellous image:

> There is a red carnation in that vase. A single flower as we sat here waiting; but now a seven-sided flower, many-petalled, red, puce, purple-shaded, stiff with silver-tinted leaves, a whole flower to which every eye brings its own contribution.

Yet as we have seen, this 'moment' is thoroughly hedged with qualification and transience, and by the same token the suggested merger or union of the six friends into a larger being exists more as an aspiration than a sustained achievement. Throughout this scene, and even more strongly at Hampton Court, there is a sense of strain, a feeling of being contained not just by time, but by the contexts of individual identity. The fact is of course that such 'poetic' doubling as Woolf wants to appropriate is far more difficult to attain in fiction, precisely because the 'realistic' contexts of 'life itself' inhibit a transcendent suggestion. Blake's difficulty in suggesting a mythic level was considerably lessened by the fact that both his figures and the world in which they move are already totally mythopoetic. Woolf, however, remains enough of a novelist to want to convey a sense of common experience and her characters are set firmly against a background of the actual world. Woolf has tried to get around this problem by keeping her figures 'abstract' and essential, using the various formal and stylistic devices examined in the third chapter. But even so, they cannot escape the particularity of fictional characters – indeed it is remarkable how quickly we adjust to the conventions the book establishes and begin seeing the six protagonists as distinct individuals. Their engagement with the 'stream' of life, however distanced or displaced, places them inescapably in the flux of real existence. We see the effort and the suggestion they make towards the larger dimension of 'a single complete person' at such moments, but they cannot fully achieve it – the mimetic forestalls the mythic. Hence both dinners end with the crash of a wave back into distinct identity, and the splitting up and departure of the group.

This inadequate or incomplete union in life, however,

serves only to throw additional weight on Bernard's final soliloquy where, as has already been suggested, the most complete and successful union of the six takes place. The final theatre of their entry into a fully realized mythic dimension is the imagination, as Blake might have predicted. We have said that Bernard's imaginative re-constitution of their lives effects the final unification of the six friends, but this is a greater and more intense unity than any before. As he pursues the 'one true story' throughout this section, and we sense a growing coherence, the six lives are drawn together in a 'globe' or imaginative unity greater than any they could ever possess in life. This sense reaches a climax after Bernard describes his experience of undergoing an eclipse of the sun, which is effectively the extinction of the ego, the death of the self (a final unity would of course necessitate an escape from the confines of personality), and after emerging from this experience Bernard reaches a clarified perspective which embraces them all:

And now I ask, 'Who am I?' I have been talking of Bernard, Neville, Jinny, Susan, Rhoda and Louis. Am I all of them? Am I one and distinct? I do not know . . . Yet I cannot find any obstacle separating us. There is no division between me and them. As I talked I felt 'I am you.' This difference we make so much of, this identity we so feverishly cherish, was overcome . . . Here on my brow is the blow I got when Percival fell. Here on the nape of my neck is the kiss Jinny gave Louis. My eyes fill with Susan's tears. I see far away, quivering like a gold thread, the pillar Rhoda saw, and feel the rush of the wind of her flight when she leapt.

In *Mrs Dalloway*, Woolf had attempted to suggest something similar, when near the end of the book Clarissa had sympathetically fathomed the 'essence' of Septimus Smith's life, and thus the reasons for his suicide, as a result of which she had similarly lost her identity and joined together with him in a 'moment' of mystical union. Here Woolf has taken the process much further; Bernard absorbs the lives of all the others and in the process initiates a swelling 'globe' of understanding: 'Immeasurably receptive, holding everything, trembling with fullness, yet clear, contained – so my being seems.' This causes him to expand beyond the confines of identity and prepares the way for the denouement of the book, for the 'moment of being' working here is accompanied by a distinct and unmistakable sense of elevation:

Now to-night, my body rises tier upon tier like some cool temple, whose floor is strewn with carpets and murmurs rise and the altars stand smoking; but up above, here in my serene head, come only fine gusts of melody, waves of incense . . .

Absorbing everything in the book, Bernard experiences an enormous imaginative expansion; 'looking down from this transcendency' he perceives the clarified shape of human life and thus begins to gesture toward a mythic stature, becoming a modern version of Everyman or a representation of humanity itself. It is in this light that the scale of his final heroic act of 'defiance' (pitching himself on the mythic plane) becomes clear:

And in me too the wave rises. It swells; it arches its back. I am aware once more of a new desire, something rising beneath me like the proud horse whose rider first spurs then pulls him back. What enemy do we now perceive advancing against us, you whom I ride now, as we stand pawing this stretch of pavement? It is death. Death is the enemy. It is death against whom I ride with my spear couched and my hair flying back like a young man's, like Percival's, when he galloped in India. I strike spurs into my horse. Against you I will fling myself, unvanquished and unyielding, O Death!

His last act is an heroic one (like the heroes of Greek epic), where he rises out of all mimetic or realistic contexts to suggest a figure of all humankind, spurred by its unquenchable will to the effort of resistance, making a defiant last stand against the ultimate human enemy, Death.

Before we leave this particular aspect of the book, it is as well to note one other sense in which the six characters are one – a sense that sharpens the focus on the author. We have seen that Woolf intended the sextet to be 'all different', and so in one sense they are. But there are similarities which counteract such distinctions, the most obvious being the indistinguishable style. As many critics have observed, the six characters all speak the same language. That is to say, they all employ the same 'poetic' devices of parallelisms, repetitions, metaphorical passion, ellisions, etc., often sharing the same key phrases or words. An undifferentiated high style unites them all. James Naremore has finely observed that this stylistic similarity suggests their metaphysical unity; but it is also true that the six share the same *voice* – highly strung, nervous, with a persistent lyricism which does not conceal an underlying urgency. Numerous critics have pointed to the fact that it is a tone of voice which closely resembles the eloquent, literary, helpless narrator of the early short stories ('The Mark on the Wall', 'An Unwritten Novel') and *Jacob's Room*. Here of course style follows substance, since the fact is they all share an intense self-consciousness, being hyper-aware of their own actions and experience, and bent always on analysing that experience. More and more we may be reminded of the accents of Virginia Woolf's diary. The search for 'it', we remember, engendered 'a sense of my own strangeness . . . Who am I, what am I, & so on', which is continually reflected in the characters' own speech, for example Louis: 'Rippling and questioning begin. What do I think of you – what do you think of me? Who are you? Who am I? – that quivers again its uneasy air over us.' As the book goes on it becomes increasingly clear that the six characters are imbued with much of their creator's searching self-consciousness, absorbing something of her own metaphysical urgency; they are all looking for 'some discovery in life', something they can lay hands on and say 'this is it', without fully knowing what 'it' is. And this similarity among the six anxious questors ultimately comes to seem far more 'essential' than the surface distinctions in their characteristics.

A further point which might be made in this connection is that all the characters in *The Waves* come, quite patently, from the same social class. Not only in their extremely articulate and 'literary' speech, but in their various haunts of public school, Cambridge, museums, concert halls, restaurants, they betray their place in the intellectual, upper-middle class to which Virginia Woolf herself belonged. Unbeknown to her, the book tells us a great deal about 'the houses, incomes, occupations of its characters', albeit indirectly; there is perhaps as much 'material' indication in *The Waves* as in any work of Arnold Bennett, though of course not as explicit. This is quite simply because Woolf, no more than any writer, could not surmount her own time and situation; in attempting to create 'universal' characteristics she has necessarily drawn on her own experience, and projected aspects of that time and situation into her creation. Though the aim of *The Waves* was to universalize experience, it quickly becomes apparent that these six could not really yield the 'life of anyone'; they are too clearly a composite of the 'life of Bloomsbury' – or more precisely, of Virginia Woolf herself.

The more we read, the clearer it seems that Woolf has projected much of herself into her six characters. This notion is considerably reinforced by Woolf's personal writings; not only her diary but her recently published autobiographical writings reveal some astonishing links. In the originating diary entry Woolf had sought to clarify the 'essence of reality' by recalling an incident from her childhood when she could not cross a puddle for thinking 'Who am I', and this has been transposed wholly into the text, when Rhoda entertains the following reflection on her school days; 'Also in the middle, cadaverous, awful, lay the grey puddle in the courtyard . . . I came to the puddle. I could not cross. Identity failed me.' An even more striking example of such biographical transference occurs in the first section when the child Neville comes up against death for the first time:

I heard about the dead man through the swingdoor last night when the cook was shoving in and out the dampers. He was found with his throat cut. The apple-tree leaves became fixed in the sky; the moon glared; I was unable to lift my foot up the stair. He was found in the gutter. His blood gurgled down the gutter. His jowl was white as a dead codfish. I shall call this structure, this rigidity, 'death among the apple trees' for ever. There were the floating pale-grey clouds; and the immitigable tree; the implacable tree with its greaved silver bark. The ripple of my life was unavailing. I was unable to pass by. There was an obstacle. 'I cannot surmount this unintelligible obstacle,' I said. And the others passed on. But we are doomed, all of us . . . by the immitigable tree which we cannot pass.

The intensity of this piece of writing derives from Woolf's personal experience: in her autobiographical piece, 'A Sketch of the Past', she describes a series of 'shocks' she experienced as a child, one of the strongest being when she too first encountered death:

Some people called Valpy had been staying at St Ives and had left. We were waiting at dinner one night, when somehow I overheard my father or my mother say that Mr Valpy had killed himself. The next thing I can remember is being in the garden at night and walking on the path by the apple tree. It seemed to me that the apple tree was connected with the horror of Mr Valpy's suicide. I could not pass it. I stood there looking at the grey-green creases of its back − it was a moonlit night − in a trance of horror. I seemed to be dragged down, into some pit of absolute despair from which I could not escape. My body seemed paralysed.

Virginia Woolf may have desired to 'practise anonymity', in this book, to get beyond her own personality, but such direct investment as these examples suggest reveals she was not wholly successful in the enterprise. The further we probe, the clearer this becomes. Woolf's note that 'London itself perpetually attracts, stimulates, gives me a play & a story and a poem, without any trouble, save that of moving my legs through the streets' (31 May 1928) is directly quoted when Neville likens London to Shakespeare − 'If it were only for the sake of the play, I could walk Shaftesbury Avenue for ever'. Bernard too is strongly drawn to the actual world, which leads to his inveterate 'phrase-making', attempting to fix the moment in an arresting phrase − a habit which also marked his author: 'The look of things has a great power over me. Even now, I watch the rooks beating up against the wind, which is high, & still I say to myself instinctively ''Whats the phrase for that?'' ' (12 Aug. 1928). Examples could be multiplied, for the fact is the work is 'saturated' with 'personality'. Under the appearance of invention lies a core of memory, and, through the guise of Bloomsbury portraits, Woolf has effectively projected six different versions of herself. Thus Jinny is a project of Woolf's love of clothes and social occasions; Susan, under cover of maternal passion (based on her sister, Vanessa), Woolf's love of the Sussex Downs and country life; Neville, under guise of Lytton Strachey, her love of London and literature; Rhoda's terror of crowds and hatred of her body an almost too close realization of that 'other' Virginia Woolf, the schizophrenic; Louis's intense ordering, her own love of poetry and fear of transience; and Bernard, her deepest love of 'life itself' and the attempt to put into words. Her letter to G. L. Dickinson makes this suggestion patent:

The six characters were supposed to be one. I'm getting old myself . . . and I come to feel more and more how difficult it is to collect oneself in Virginia; even though the special Virginia in whose body I live at the moment is violently susceptible to all sorts of separate feelings.

Behind their awareness that 'we are not single, we are one' lies not only a mythic suggestion of humanity itself, but a personal one of their creator's attempt 'to collect oneself in Virginia', imaginatively to unify all the 'separate feelings' of which she was possessed. The subtitle of *The Waves* might very well be 'six characters in search of an author', which is of course what Bernard becomes in the final soliloquy. We have said that his 'telling the story' of their lives on one occasion means that he has taken over the role of that shadowy original narrator, which now comes to seem perilously close to the perspective of the author. J. W. Graham observed that the sibylline narrator presented Woolf with several problems of point of view; as she wrote in her diary, the difficulty became 'Who thinks it? And am I outside the thinker?' (25 Sept. 1929). In fact she found it difficult to keep such an omniscient figure, stuffed with her own reflections and experiences, from becoming a transparent mask for herself, so she expunged this narrator and divided her function among the characters. But when Bernard reunites the parts in the final soliloquy, that resemblance returns; when he presents us with the filled and completed globe of 'my life', it is hard not to see the author herself speaking, offering the reader an imaginatively coherent and shaped account of *her* life. This may have been the reason why she switched sexes, changing her original idea of the 'semi-mystic very profound life of a *woman*' (my italics) telling the story, giving the final summing up to Bernard, his maleness being another disguise. In any event the 'single complete person' hovering behind the book is surely on one level the author herself, and the ebb and flow of the larger being they all sense that they represent is also the rhythm of Woolf's 'personality' entering the work.

Chapter 5

The novel and *The Waves*

Our detailed examination of *The Waves* has uncovered many of the book's salient features – in particular its formal, abstracting drive to move away from novelistic conventions, its structural division between the sensitive and insensitive, human awareness and 'what we are not', and its thematic tension between stasis and process, the meaningful 'moment' and 'life itself going on'. With a grasp of these essentials, we can now refine some of the points raised in the analysis and consider some interesting and unusual perspectives suggested by the work, in particular its complex and ambiguous relation to 'the novel'.

The plot of narrative

It is often said that *The Waves* has no plot in the ordinary novelistic sense. This observation is linked with the fact that few of Woolf's novels, at least her modernist or experimental works, have much in the way of a 'story'. An ageing Westminster hostess plans and throws a party, a group of summer residents gather in a house by the sea, a village pageant is put on one summer afternoon – such is the unadventurous basis of some of her most famous works. Thus Elizabeth Hardwick's claim that for all their formal extravagance Woolf's novels 'aren't interesting', a view echoed by those critics who charge that 'nothing happens' in a Woolf novel. They mean of course that any sense of action or event in the work is trivial compared with the emphasis which is thrown on the internal, mental sphere; there is no 'story' in the usual sense since all the weight has been placed on the 'luminous halo' of consciousness. 'Don't bother about the plot – the plot's nothing' says one of the characters in

Between the Acts, and the remark has often been applied wholesale to Virginia Woolf's 'serious poetic experimental' work. This is a simplification of what actually takes place since, as we have seen, there is a sustained dramatic conflict between inner and outer levels of experience; but relative to more robustly plotted fiction the observation does have some force. We might think that the exteriorized speakers in *The Waves* would do better, but here the sense of actual events is held even further off, and in those static and stylized devices of *The Waves* the traditional notion of 'story' seems to dissolve entirely. Even so, matters are more complicated than this, and the whole issue of 'plot' rises in a complex and challenging way.

When dealing with fundamental literary components such as plot, it is sensible to return to Aristotle for a solid ground on which to begin. In *The Poetics*, Aristotle defined plot as 'an action' which is of 'a certain magnitude', by which he means an action which is before the author in a completed whole, an entirety – hence its ability to demonstrate a beginning, middle and end. Plot is linked with the idea of integrity, of wholeness, which can be seized by the mind in an abstract, spatial way. Aristotle pressed this view of the fundamentals of literature because he wished to elevate *drama*, which conveyed the action or plot to an audience in such a way that its complete and coherent form could be easily grasped. The undercurrent throughout this discussion is an attack on narrative – he had the epic poems of Homer in mind – whose extended and episodic structure tended to draw out the plot, obscure the completed whole, and break up the coherent pattern of beginning, middle and end. The reason for this is obvious; narrative tends to throw increased emphasis on a sense of experience and process rather than completed action, to be be more like life, and less like the consonant integrity of art. It is for this reason that *The Poetics* persistently elevates drama over epic, the patterned completion of plot over the episodic process of narrative.

This antithesis was to be full of implication for the novel, which of course descends from the epic. The form depends heavily on narrative, on telling the tale, and is suffused with all the episodic structure and experiential analysis which Aristotle abhorred. Though 'plot' is a common term in discussion of the novel, it is rarely used in its Aristotelian sense, but usually taken to mean 'story', the sense of things happening in temporal sequence. However, an interesting legacy of this Aristotelian opposition occurs in E. M. Forster's *Aspects of the Novel*, which similarly distinguishes between *plot* (the 'story in its intellectual aspect', a sense of completed form) and *story* (the progress of the tale, 'what happens' in the text). The latter category includes the concept of narrative, or how the story is presented or told, and most formal analysis of fiction follows suit (as in the current narratological division between 'story' and 'discourse', defined by Jonathan Culler as 'a basic distinction between a sequence of events and a discourse that orders and presents events'). The interest of Forster's book is that it conducts a sustained counterattack on Aristotle's theory, debunking the notion of patterned form inherent in a well-made plot (which on this view belongs to drama) and championing the sense of experience and process in the novel. The novel, Forster argues, is the more wayward, humane, and 'life-like' form, and to be defended for this reason.

At the time Forster was writing, however, this argument already had a defensive and reactionary air to it. For the devotion to narrative, like the novel itself, had blossomed through the eighteenth and nineteenth centuries, where the narrator had become an ever-stronger, more dominant and palpable force, contributing to the reassuring sense of stability and order in such fiction. By the early twentieth century, a full-scale reaction to this development was under way. Modern fiction became involved in an attempt to get away from the novel's emphasis on narrative story-telling, as one can see in the various attempts to remove or depress the narrator. Joyce's Flaubertian ideal that the author should stand outside his creation, removed, indifferent, paring his fingernails, like God everywhere felt but nowhere present, set the tone for much of the modernist experiments in fiction.

Indeed much of this trend can be seen as moving away from 'the novel' and returning to *drama*, as the influence of Ibsen on Joyce and the reiterated 'dramatic' ideal of Henry James's prefaces suggest. What is implied here is clearly a desire to return to the Aristotelian notion of plot, reducing the element of process so as to bring out the patterned, coherent whole. Joseph Frank's classic essay, 'Spatial Form in Modern Literature', deals with precisely this development. The ideal of integral whole, of coherent pattern or form, is an aesthetic one, which shifts the emphasis from life to art, and the aesthetic intensification of modern fiction has one source in Henry James, whose prefaces insist on the notion of making action intense, clarifying and crystallizing 'life' into an ordered whole. This may explain why Forster makes a particularly petulant attack on James in *Aspects of the Novel*; but the pendulum in modernist fiction was swinging away from Forster's choice and back towards an earlier, classical idea.

The modernist Virginia Woolf was of course caught up in this swing, and nowhere more so than in *The Waves*. As explored in the second chapter above, that 'furthest development so far' was engaged in a concerted move away from the 'narrative business' of the novel towards the more 'concentrated', 'abstract' ideal of drama. Woolf's post-ulations in 'The Narrow Bridge of Art' were consonant with a larger trend of the time. This clearly implied a shift towards 'plot' in Aristotle's sense, depressing the 'story'; and the abstraction of the characters from their own lives is a corresponding move in the same direction. Yet as we have also seen, that sense of time and the river which is inherent in the story could not be wholly excluded, but continues to enter the work. In this sense 'story' and 'plot', the experiential and the abstract, contend against one another in the work, a contest which is focused by Virginia Woolf's treatment of narrative.

J. W. Graham's essay, to which I have already referred, deals at length with Woolf's struggle with her initial conception of a 'semi-mystic very profound life of a woman', which would be told on one occasion and obliterate time. This notion was taken in a mystical direction by casting this female narrator as a shadowy *vates* figure who saw and was 'telling [herself] the story of the world from the beginning', a tale which incorporates and progressively centres on the lives of the six characters. As Graham details, this conception put an increasing strain on Virginia Woolf, because the dramatized narrator always threatened to become the centre of interest and Woolf's struggle to keep her sufficiently vague and 'impersonal' was fraught with awkward and stilted effects, of which she was perfectly conscious: 'But who is she? I am very anxious that she should have no name. I don't want a Lavinia or a Penelope: I want "She". But that becomes arty, Liberty greenery yallery somehow: symbolic in loose robes' (28 May 1929). This was precisely the stilted and unreal effect for which she had castigated the modern poetic play in 'The Narrow Bridge of Art', and her own 'mystical' impulse was now taking her in the same direction. Moreover, there was a constant threat, in keeping the central narrative voice so unrealized, that it would be confused with the author herself, a point of which she was also well aware: 'Who thinks it? And am I outside the thinker? One wants some device which is not a trick' (25 Sept. 1929). This possibility was especially threatening given her desire to move beyond personality in the work. In the end, therefore, she settled the matter by expunging the dramatized narrator completely and resolving the characters' lives 'into a series of dramatic soliloquies'. The characters themselves absorbed the burden of the original narrator completely, which explains why they are always speaking.

The result of this move is to 'saturate' the work with narrative. The speaking voices drone on with a narrative fervour which outdoes any Victorian novel, since it swallows up entirely their actual existence; they are wholly engaged with 'telling' rather than showing, and the narration is foregrounded so intensely that the 'events' of their lives virtually disappear. Their fluent speech, which suspends them from time, suspends them from 'plot' as well, since any sense of sustained or completed action dissolves under pressure of the sustained narrative process the soliloquies put on it. And yet, there surely is a 'plot' in this book, one of the oldest and most 'essential' of all plots: birth, growth, development, change, death. This is a very complete and coherent action with a beginning, middle and end, so clear it can hardly be missed. Though from time to time the characters call attention to this overtly, the temporal plot usually exists as a covert pressure which, as we have seen, emanates from the interludes. Here we see yet another function of the structure, for it is clear that the 'plot', the 'story in its intellectual aspect' is contained in the solar interludes. The 'action' which disappears in the stream of narrative is condensed in the interludes, which show the completed form of a single day. In this sense, the 'plot' exerts a constant pressure on the narrative which has expelled it. The narrative obscures and dissolves plot, but plot channels and contains narrative; and we can also see that through the expanded narrative the characters conduct a campaign to hold off that 'sense of an ending', the inevitable closure which the *completed* action of plot entails. That ending is of course *their* ending, or death, and the last line of the book, 'The waves broke on the shore', is the completion of the plot, which the speakers have struggled valiantly to hold off.

In this work, then, the 'essential' components of the novel are divided and in contest. The thematic tension between the mind and the sun, sensitive and insensitive nature, voice and silence, is also that ancient war between narrative and plot. She has split the novel along its 'essential' fault line and set the two halves against one another; the wave-like engagement which they pursue takes the struggle with 'the novel' to intense and more abstract heights.

The time of story

As narrative is such a crucial element in the book it is worth trying to analyze some of its features more closely, and to this end I shall draw on some of the structuralist analyses of

Gerard Genette, which I think are especially useful here. Perhaps it is worth observing that Woolf herself was not especially theoretical, or even very interested in what we now think of as literary theory. She did, it is true, strive to develop new concepts in the practice of fiction, and she expounded these in discursive form; but her approach to this was largely instinctive, and the commentary of her diary and essays remains impressionistic and sketchy rather than precise. She recognized, sometimes with regret, her 'lack of intellectual power', but even so she had no taste for the kind of systermatic theorizing which has overtaken the study of fiction today. Her approach to critical matters was largely that of her father — balanced, sane, drawing on a wealth of shared knowledge in a cultural tradition and addressed to the 'common reader'. This does not mean that she was uninterested in formal matters, still less that her works are formally uninteresting. It does mean that she will not prove a guide to any rigorous description of her technical features. In the case of *The Waves* her narrative technique is particularly problematic, and one which greatly benefits from the analytical approach of Genette. Through employing some of his key concepts and terms we can begin to get a tighter grip on the fluid texture of *The Waves*, and see more clearly how the narrative which seeks to counteract plot ultimately confirms it.

Genette follows standard structuralist practice by dividing fiction into 'story' and 'discourse', which effectively repeat the categories of plot and narrative in the preceding discussion. 'Story' here is always used to mean the action or events in temporal order, and 'discourse' the narrational manipulation of these events. It is thus important that in employing this method of analysis we keep the notion of 'story' associated with the term 'plot' and separate from narrative process. Genette divides his analysis of narrative into three broad categories, each yielding numerous subcategories. To follow through all of these with regard to *The Waves* would be a formidable undertaking and require more space than we have here. However, for our purposes the most useful category is that of Time, which focuses on the temporal relations between narrative and story. Genette breaks this down into three sub-categories: order, duration and frequency, each of which offers interesting perspectives on *The Waves*.

Order

Writers often alter the order of events in a story; indeed often part of the challenge of a novel is to establish the story-line. In difficult works such as Conrad's *Nostromo*, for example, disentangling the proper order of events from the narrational splintering is a major part of the enterprise of reading the work. One might expect *The Waves* to be problematic in this regard, due to the sustained use of the pure present, which could conceivably collapse all events into an unmarked continuum. In her book, *The Rhetoric of the Unreal*, Christine Brooke-Rose points to just such a result in Gertrude Stein's suggestions for a 'continuous present' which would flatten out all markings of temporal order. Such suggestions, she notes, were brought to fruition in the French *nouveau roman*; the novels of Robbe-Grillet exploit the fusion of time caused by continuous present in order deliberately to confuse the order of events. As Brooke-Rose observes, his use of repeated episodes in the sustained present tense means: 'we never quite know when (and whether) something is occurring, or recurring, or being recalled'. In *The Waves*, however, such confusion does not arise. In spite of the sustained present tense, we and the characters are linked to a clear temporal progression, a steady sense of time passing – the *order* of narration is secured. The 'story' as such is the growth and development of the six, charted through a series of 'moments' in their lives – the first day at school, the arrival at College, the farewell dinner in London, the reunion at Hampton Court, etc. The story is obscured or diffused by the fact that such 'events' are swathed in narrative, to the point where they hardly exist as independent actions; and yet the shape of time shows through. This anchoring is of course partly the result of the structure, the inescapable feature of the interludes marking out the passage of time; but it is also part of the 'process' the characters realize at any one point, marking the change and development which has occurred. Hence though they are always in the enormously expansive present, the backbone of time secures the 'story' against all the dissolvent and transcendent efforts of the narrative.

Brooke-Rose is interested in transgression (the title of her chapter), in the ways in which the *nouveau roman* seeks to subvert or destroy conventional narrative modes. What is interesting about *The Waves*, however, is the way in which it courts such 'absolute' transgression but never wholly engenders it, being held back by the conventional pressures of 'story' or plot. Narrative in this work seeks the extreme, but it is *not* allowed the transgressional freedom or 'free play' over story which the *noveau roman* enjoys, even though it sometimes seems to move in this direction. The 'story', and its clear temporal link, always remain as a check and a counter to such freedom. In this sense Woolf's work is more 'traditional', a fact which justifies Brooke-Rose's horrified reaction to comparisons of Woolf to Nathalie Sarraute. Woolf's 'furthest development' in enlarging the scope of narrative is still linked to the mimetic purpose of conveying 'life itself', the stream of time in which human beings are bound. Her urge to formal experiment does not leave the 'traditional' novel entirely behind; the sustained temporal pressure of the 'story' puts *order* into the narrative of *The Waves* and shapes a more coherent work of art. Such an intent is dismissed by theorists as severe as Brooke-Rose, but it is possible to think that Woolf gains by this attachment. She has different interests and constraints in mind than the purely formal experiments of such high abstractors as Robbe-Gillet, where, as Brooke-Rose puts it, 'Nothing is "lived" except the author in his writing experience and the reader in his reading experience.' Compared with this extreme, Woolf's work retains a link with 'life itself' which make it a more humane work to read. Moreover, bound by the very conventions it wishes to escape, *The Waves* is shaped throughout by a tension between tradition and experiment, the containing forces of time and life and the uncontained urge of consciousness − a tension which makes it an altogether more paradoxical, animated and interesting work.

Duration

The second sub-category of Time is duration, which measures narrative pace − that is, how fast the narrative proceeds in relation to the story − and Genette expresses this in terms of a relation between narrative time (NT) and story-time (ST). For example, a summary, giving a condensed account of a portion of the story, is a case in which the story-time is paramount and narrative itself reduced: $NT < ST$. In scene (of which dialogue is a pure example), the two advance at the same rate: $NT = ST$. The dominant durational element of *The Waves*, interestingly enough, would appear to be what Genette claims is the 'missing' category, where the narrative time supersedes that of the story, $NT > ST$. In *The Waves* the duration of the narrative is vastly greater than that of the story, since the 'story', the event or actions, consists of a few moments or points in the characters' lives around which the 'saturated' narrative forms. The story is a bare record, the narrative an expansive plenitude. Indeed here the push is always toward what Genette calls 'descriptive pause', where the story stops entirely and narrative takes over: $NT \infty > ST$ (narrative time infinitely greater than story time). But again, the narrative never quite reaches this extreme because the 'story' never quite ceases or disappears; the link with action and events in time is diminished or obscured, but never entirely broken. 'These things happen in one second and last forever', exclaims Bernard, and this account of their experience also describes their narration. Once again the narrative is kept from the 'free play' of entirely self-sustaining discourse by the anchor of the 'story', those points in time and implied sequence of events in their lives which the narrative never completely escapes.

Frequency

Genette's final sub-category of Time is frequency, which categorizes how often the events of the story occur in the narrative. At first *The Waves* appears to be a straightforward example of the 'singulative', which is telling once what happens once. But it soon becomes clear that something else is happening, as the narrative begins to double back on itself and re-present things which have already occurred. This moves it to the 'repetitive' mode, which means telling more than once what happens once. We see this very clearly in the communal scenes; at the farewell dinner for Percival in the fourth section, the six go back over their past and re-tell the occurrences of their earlier narrative, even employing some of the same descriptive phrases. Similarly, at Hampton Court this repetitive element in the narrative recurs. By far the strongest instance of this, however, is Bernard's final summing up, when he reiterates the whole course of their lives, drawing freely upon narrative phrases which have been used already. Such overlappings, of course, emphasize the primacy of narrative over story; they highlight the fact that it is to the flexible and fluid manipulation of narrative that we are paying attention. Even so, there is a subtle countermovement here, an insurgency of the story as it were, for the very fact of the repetitions establishes those few and minimal actions or events all the more firmly. The repeated blows of the narrative disperse most of what we normally think of as the story, but also hammer home those few points of 'life' to which the reflecting consciousnesses are fixed, nailed fast as it were, and thus ensure that the animating and productive tension between them continues.

One final point which we may make in this regard is that most of what is said about the soliloquies here also holds true for the interludes, which present a second order of narration outside the reported speech of the characters. The interludes in effect recapitulate the pattern of the soliloquies, taking a single point in time and swathing it in narrative – though here both elements, the specific point in time and the narrative expansion, are pushed to an extreme to bring out the underlying principle. Recognizing this establishes an 'essential' link between the two structural parts of the book, despite all their obvious differences, and prepares the way for the most surprising development of all, when the two come together.

This union of the two narrative levels occurs in Bernard's summing up, when in the process of imaginatively absorbing everything in the book, all the 'life' which has preceded him, he achieves the final purgation of his 'own sharp absurd personality' and attains a new perspective. This development is imaged in terms of a solar eclipse, when Bernard enters a realm of total 'anonymity', glimpsing 'the world seen without a self'. This is clearly a gesture towards expressing that apprehension of 'something in the universe' which is 'not oneself', and the experience is both frightening and exciting for Bernard. However, what interests us here is his sense, after emerging from the eclipse, of having gained access to a new perspective: 'But for a moment I sat on the turf somewhere high above the flow of the sea . . . had seen the house, the garden and the waves breaking.' This, astonishingly enough, is the perspective of the interludes; Bernard has been elevated to the clarified vision of 'what we are not' which the book has been insistently counterposing to the human perspective. Just in case there is any doubt about this, in the next moment, Bernard appropriates the *voice* of the interludes as well:

Day rises; the girl lifts the watery fire-hearted jewels to her brow; the sun levels his beams straight at the sleeping house; the waves deepen their bars; they fling themselves on shore; back blows the spray; sweeping their waters they surround the boat and the sea-holly. The birds sing in chorus; deep tunnels run between the stalks of flowers; the house is whitened; the sleeper stretches; gradually all is astir.

This startling event has always been a problem in dealing with *The Waves*, and approaching the matter through Genette's analysis of narrative helps us to account for it. The other two broad categories of Genettian analysis are Mood and Voice, which have to do with classifying the narrator within narrative. Mood attempts to discriminate 'who sees' the events, and Voice 'who speaks' – not always one and the same. Both these categories when applied to *The Waves* highlight the narrative division in the work – that is to say, bring out the book's different levels of narration. At an obvious level, the perspective and voice differ between the characters' soliloquies and the impersonal narrator of the interludes; but even within the soliloquies themselves the conventions of reported speech, the sustained use of 'said', gestures towards another narrator outside the characters' awareness. J. W. Graham observes that these traces are all that remain of the original narrator of the work, that shadowy *vates* figure of Woolf's first conception, whose knowledge and percipience the characters themselves have absorbed. The vestiges which remain, however, constantly imply that this ghostly 'invisible' narrator outside the characters is the same as that impersonal and omniscient one of the interludes. The six therefore have absorbed all 'her' functions and awareness, *except* the knowledge of 'what we are not', which is in the narrative domain of the interludes. Thus when Bernard, in his summing up, finally absorbs the perspective and the knowledge of the interludes, it is effectively to cross narrative levels, what Genette calls a 'metalepsis'. Bernard in a sense becomes 'the narrator' of the entire work, taking the place of that original figure, and 'telling the story' of all. His perspective and voice expand to the highest level of the work, encompassing everything in the book. This shift adds to the sense of elevation he achieves at the climax; in the end, there is nothing outside his narrative (except of course Death). And the reverberations of his declaration that 'there is no difference between us' carry past his five fellow characters to that omniscient narrator who has hitherto contained them.

An unwritten novel

Any account of *The Waves* ought to confront a question which it constantly and implicitly raises. Before embarking on the book, Woolf said she never wanted to write another 'novel': did she succeed in this ambition? or is *The Waves* a novel after all? The question has been much debated. Many critics have found this 'a radically a-novelistic work' and concluded that efforts to read it as a novel are pointless. There are good reasons for taking such a view, some of which we have explored in the previous sections. Yet the issue cannot be disposed of so easily. The presence of 'the novel' haunts *The Waves* in a particularly interesting way.

All of the analysis we have undertaken thus far has served to highlight the work's problematic relation to 'the novel'. It contains, as we have seen, many standard novelistic features − a strong narrative base, a defined temporal structure, elements of character, plot and setting. But each of these features is abstracted or estranged, presented at a remove. In the same way that the characters are suspended above the events of their own lives, *The Waves* seems to hover above a 'novel', always pointing to what it is removed from. It seems to both approach and withdraw from its status as a novel, so that there is a tension throughout between the suggestion and the denial. Part of the cause of this effect may be traceable to its intention, the original purpose to convey 'the essence of reality'. Metaphysics moves beyond fiction, forcing a compression or reduction to an 'essential' state through the various formal astringencies we have examined. Yet one of the most interesting aspects of the book is the rearguard action by "novel". It is remarkable how quickly we adjust to the temperature of *The Waves* and become used to the strange conventions it employs. The six figures quickly become read as 'characters', their progress through the world as a 'story', and, as we have seen, the sense of process of 'life itself' soon makes its way back against the detaching form. We could say that the fictional element of the work is in an antagonistic relation to the metaphysical, generating a large tension which keeps the whole book on the stretch.

This view of *The Waves* is confirmed by its evolution. We saw earlier how the book was borne on a reaction against 'the novel', a further stage in Woolf's long-standing dis-satisfaction with the form, and her modernist efforts to change it. This nourished a devotion to abstraction and stylization which would enhance its formal, 'poetic' character, reducing the conventionally mimetic element in the interests of abstract art. The impetus for this was increased by the extremely remote and 'mystical' nature of her original inspiration – the vision of a fin passing far out which suggested 'the essence of reality'. She tried to frame 'these mystical feelings' in the strange and severe form of 'a mind thinking', a static, shadowy and sibylline figure who told herself 'the story of the world from the beginning'. And yet, as our examination has revealed, the final form of the work did not sustain such a pure or 'abstract' ambition. What occurred was what we might call a steady 'novelization' of that original conception, fleshing it out in more conventionally fictional dress – a strengthening of character which displaced the insubstantial narrator, an increasing condensation of plot, and most of all a reassertion of the elemental 'stream' of 'life itself', of the narrative 'process' or episodic progression through experience which is central to the novel.

All of these developments served to counteract the stark and ascetic thrust of her original ambitions and suggest that ultimately Woolf was too much of a novelist to sustain such pure abstraction. The fact of the matter is that, like Mrs Dalloway, she loved life. The testament to this is writ large in her Diary, which is in great part a record of her 'great content' in life, her endless curiosity about human beings, her delight in the pageant and spectacle of 'life itself'. To read her critical essays is to see the same standard applied to the great classic works of fiction she admired, and to gain some insight why, for all her dissatisfaction with the form of the novel, she continued to practice the art herself. Her attack on 'the novel' was often a displeasure with a too facile or conventional practice which robbed this sense of the richness and diversity of life. Even 'The Narrow Bridge of Art' serves to reinforce this perception, for in that essay the new form she pleads for is quite clearly a new form of 'the novel'; at the end of her demands for an infusion of poetry and drama, she suddenly rescues (or in current jargon 'recuperates') the novel, claiming (in language which might have been appropriated from Henry James) that the 'poetic' intensification she has in mind must be joined with 'the precious prerogatives of the democratic art of prose', with 'its freedom, its fearlessness, its flexibility', so as to give 'the sneer, the contrast, the question, the closeness and complexity of life'. Thus the reflective meditations of the characters of *The Waves*, while distanced from actual experience, manage to convey a tremendous sense of the varied panoply of 'life itself'. We see this, for example, in the balance between reflection and observation which the soliloquies achieve; the opening speeches suggest that the six characters' reflective awareness of life is rooted in precise focus on detail, and this acute sense of the things of this world only increases, so that, however abstruse their meditations, they are always anchored to the world:

I love punctually at ten to come into my room; I love the purple glow of the dark mahogany; I love the table and its sharp edge; and the smooth-running drawers . . .   (Louis)

There are no lights in any of the houses. There is a line of chimney-pots against the sky; and a street lamp or two burning, as lamps burn when nobody needs them . . . There is no one coming or going in this street; the day is over. A few policemen stand at the corner. Yet night is beginning.   (Jinny)

It is for this reason that the novelist Bernard is given the final task of summing up rather than the poet Louis, for we are told that Louis's condensing summary of the group 'will not be enough'. The novelist in Virginia Woolf could not be denied, any more than 'the novel' could be left out of her work.

Are we then justified in seeing the book as a novel? To do so would be to discount too much the abstracting and formal pressures which work so continuously in the book. *The Waves* both is and is not a 'novel'; it is 'unwritten' in the sense of being continually undone, re-created and dispelled, like the shape made by the waves. The work is perhaps best seen as an effort to hold off the realization of a form which Woolf wanted to go beyond, but which her imagination could not abandon; this is what I meant when I said the presence of the novel haunts *The Waves*. The interplay between process and form, narrative and plot is relevant here, for the novel of course stands at the centre of such a split. Looked at in this light what Woolf has done in this work is to atomize the novel and set its component parts against one another. The 'novel' thus becomes analogous to the 'single complete person' represented by the group, a larger body toward which the constituent elements are gesturing; the novel is glimpsed or suggested in the counterplay of opposed elements, eternally formed and dispersed in the wave-like contention of narrative and form.

If we were to take this division to the largest and most general level, we would find a fundamental tension between life and art. Traditionally the novel has been seen as the literary form most 'like life', less artificial than poetry or drama, imbued with a prosaic devotion to the common experience of human beings immersed in the world. This meant that for some while the novel was cold-shouldered as being too common and unrefined for 'art'. But in the latter part of the nineteenth century there began a reaction against this conception, an urge to emphasize the novel's status as art, its formal demands, its artificial nature, its aesthetic order and coherence. Woolf is at the late end of this movement, but she also inherited the paradox that while underlining the sense of a complete whole, the novel must also convey the sense of experiential process. This paradox (which circulates endlessly through critical discussion of the novel) is at the heart of *The Waves*.

Not surprisingly, the matter is focused on Bernard, the putative novelist of the group. He of all the characters has the greatest devotion to 'life', being endlessly curious about it, perpetually attracted to the world. But he is also perpetually engaged in 'making up stories', trying to capture experiences in phrases, 'retrieving them from formlessness with words' – in short, giving form to the 'stream' of life itself. This is of course the point at issue in his final soliloquy. Throughout the book he fills 'innumerable notebooks with phrases to be used when I have found the true story, the one story to which all these phrases refer'. This one true story would be the final fruit of art's refinement of life, the purged and condensed 'essence' or coherent shape of their lives. Early on in the book, Bernard apprehends that he will be 'called upon to provide, some winter's night, a meaning for all my observations — a line that runs from one to another, a summing up that completes'. This 'summing up' is of course his last speech, an aesthetic act of clarification, tracing the 'line that runs from one to another', and giving that completion. We have already examined how his sympathetic imagination allows him to absorb all the other lives and enable his 'shaping spirit' to work. One way of looking at *The Waves* then is to see this final soliloquy as the 'novel' of the book, an imaginative act which puts the preceding eight sections of 'life' into ordered and coherent shape. Rising to his task at the last, the novelist unites the disparate experiences of his fellow characters, just as he joins the severed halves of process and plot, life and form.

The difficulty with this reading, attractive though it is, is the tremendous provisionality and skepticism which surrounds this summary. For Bernard is also aware that 'I have never yet found that story. And I begin to ask Are there stories?' Do the 'stories' he makes, that is, have any correspondence with reality? The implication that they do not is much in evidence at the outset of his final soliloquy, where he says that all his life he has told stories and 'none of them are true'; 'stories', that is, involve a falsification and distortion of 'life itself':

. . . like children we tell each other stories, and to decorate them we make up ridiculous, flamboyant, beautiful phrases. How tired I am of stories, how tired I am of phrases that come down beautifully with all their feet on the ground! Also, how I distrust neat designs of life that are drawn upon half-sheets of note-paper. I begin to long for some little language such as lovers use, broken words, inarticulate words, like the shuffling of feet on the pavement.

The 'process' or 'stream' of 'life itself', in other words, cannot be contained in 'neat designs'. Bernard's awareness here colours the whole of the last speech; what dawns on him now is that 'life is not susceptible perhaps to the treatment we give it when we try to tell it'; the 'globe' he makes in this last soliloquy is to the last an 'illusion'. Hence his repeated confessions of failure, his ever-present sense of the impossibility of giving a 'complete' account of life, and his awareness of the partial and fragmentary record of his friends' lives — a judgement we can measure in comparing the previous eight sections with his final rendering. 'Life' in this sense undermines art; the novel remains unwritten. As Bernard undertakes to tell the one true story he is overwhelmed by the contingent nature of the enterprise; at the moment when he rises to his full height and purports to complete 'the novel', he confesses that it is impossible. Life *has* no 'shape' — 'of story, of design, I do not see a trace' — and the effort to impose one is an abstraction, a simplification, an 'illusion'. It is an old paradox, but one which is taken seriously here: art is a lie.

Bernard's situation is his author's, and the tension he feels here was her burden throughout the book. Woolf's skepticism about the fiction-making enterprise is a persistent element in her thought. In the summer of 1926 she wrote in her diary that 'the greatest book in the world' would be one which 'was made entirely and solely with the integrity of one's thoughts. Suppose one could catch them before they became "works of art"?' Here is a similar longing for an unmediated reality, for a 'little language' which would rescue the actual from its fictional distortion. An urge to convey 'the essence of reality', what exists outside human arrangement, would reinforce this, and pursuing the aim meant that Woolf's struggle became one to dramatize 'life itself' without the falsifying arrangements of art, and the tremendous sense of 'process' in the book which resists the formal arrangements springs from this source. Yet it quickly becomes clear that the dark side of this desire is a flood of mere process, a formless and undifferentiated stream, and Woolf was equally possessed by the desire for 'effort' and resistance, of which, as we saw, art was the chief means. The abstracting and cohering powers in the book stem from this source. Life has no shape, but the human need to find one is omnipresent: this is the 'essential' paradox to which *The Waves* is committed. If the tracing of pattern or design in life is an illusion, it is all Bernard has in the end with which to 'oppose' the 'formless imbecility' of existence — and this of course is why he goes ahead and makes the attempt in the final speech. Art is a lie, but it is an essential one — truth lies in a fiction, as Wallace Stevens put it. *The Waves* holds hard to both sides of the paradox, which stretches the tension in a book which entertains the contradictory ideal to at once 'put everything in' and 'eliminate all waste'. Bernard in this last section thus becomes a focus for Virginia Woolf's own dilemma, caught between a Scylla of form and a Charybdis of formlessness.

Finally, however, the way in which both aspirations are contained is the achievement of the book. *The Waves* treads a fine line between coherence and disorder, meaning and formlessness. The essential drama of the work is the way in which order and coherence are suggested despite being continually broken up and dispersed. There is, unmistakably, a sense of the confusing and fluid 'stream' of life in the book, but also an ordered and 'essential' presentation of it in a coherent form. The same paradox is visible in the conclusion itself, for even as Bernard confesses his uncertainty and distrust about the task, he makes the 'effort'; he does 'tell the story' of the lives we have just read and puts the confusing and contradictory nature of experience into a 'shape'. We do get a sense of a 'summing up' here, an intimation of coherence, however provisional and contingent. The summary, the artful 'globe' of their cumulative experience does suggest a 'novel' — though of course it too is an 'unwritten novel', ending as it began in the contingency of speech. There are a number of conflicting thrusts and counterthrusts in the summary, which holds off any complete formal condensation; but nevertheless we do gain a 'momentary' sense of 'roundness, weight, depth, and completion'.

And the same is true, at a larger remove, of the work as a whole. Like Bernard's last soliloquy, the book itself suggests a shape of human life emerging out of the welter it encloses. *The Waves* is the written version of the novel, thus more secure than Bernard's hesitant and provisional attempt. One can understand Woolf's feelings that she had 'netted the fin' of her vision. The conclusion of the book manages a nice balance of skepticism and affirmation, of the 'stream' of life with 'islands of light' within it, of temporal process and a 'moment' of coherence. This was true to the original nature of the inspiring vision, for that 'fin in a waste of water' was a momentary apparition, a sudden, inspiring appearance in the undistinguished sea. Ultimately the question of 'the novel' in the book is best looked at in the same way, a momentary appearance in the equilibrium between essence and abstraction, process and form. Woolf once said that 'one can't write directly about the soul. Looked at, it vanishes; but look at the ceiling, at Grizzle, at the beasts in the Zoo which are exposed to the walkers in Regent's Park, & the soul slips in' (27 Feb. 1926). No other account comes closer to describing the 'art' of this work, or the location of 'the novel'.

Chapter 6

The rhythm of the waves

'Now to sum up . . .' Bernard's resigned tone as he surveys the hopeless nature of his task carries its warning to the critic. Attempts to 'interpret' *The Waves*, in the sense of tracing the 'one true story' of the book, are fated to come to grief – here character and reader are one. The work has been purposely designed to frustrate the enterprise it invites, which is perhaps one of the most critically interesting things about it.

Our examination of *The Waves* has repeatedly touched upon what may well seem the most obvious feature of the book – that is, the difficulty of taking bearings within its too-fluent texture. There is no doubt that this was a highly deliberate effect. Throughout the latter stages of composition, Virginia Woolf indicated that she was writing to a 'rhythm', and of course this could only be 'the rhythm of the waves' (20 Aug. 1930). The change of title from *The Moths* was not fortuitous, but rather an 'essential' clarification; the 'rhythm' she wished to sound through the book was the systole – diastole movement of the waves, the repeated pattern of surge and ebb. We have seen, throughout this analysis, some of the ways in which that pattern manifests itself: realism and 'reality', process and meaning, life and art, narrative and plot, personality and impersonality, the individual and the group, speaker and interlude, sensitive and insensitive nature, the mind and the sun, the flowing 'stream' of life and meditative 'islands of light' – all of these dualities meet and contend in the book. It is not so much a dialectic as a constant pattern of alternation and overlap which gives the effect Woolf was trying for: 'one wave after another' (1 May 1930).

Grasping this pattern helps to explain why the book is at once so clear and confusing; for while the separate elements are clearly distinguished, their synthesis in an overall 'sum' is not. Just the reverse, for the effect is constantly to break down any coherent meaning. The difficulty is that *every* position is undermined in the work, each statement is balanced by a counterstatement, every current checked by a cross current. This is evident at once on the large scale, in the six different perspectives on experience to which we are continually subjected — Jinny's love of the body opposed to Rhoda's loathing of it, Louis's desire for solitude countering Bernard's love of company, and so forth. But it is also apparent within an individual speaker too, for example in Bernard's ambivalent attraction to personal identity and his desire to escape it. The specific points are very clear, evidence of Woolf's 'clearing, sharpening and making the good phrases shine', but the line between them becomes increasingly harder to detect as the book goes on, and the 'rhythm of the waves' effaces it.

To read the book then is to experience a constant rise and fall, to be immersed in the sense of conflicting currents and endlessly appearing and disappearing patterns, all of which serve to obscure a sense of the whole. The overdetermination leads to indeterminacy. In *To the Lighthouse* one of the characters observes that 'nothing is simply one thing', that our perceptions of reality change with time and distance. *The Waves* has taken this message to heart and 'saturated' the book with its effects; in seeking 'the essence of reality' Woolf has portrayed the radical multiplicity of experience, and 'concentrated' the essentially indeterminate aspect of 'life itself'. Here Woolf's modernist side is at its height, for in this sense *The Waves* is an extremely skeptical work, one which allows for no conclusions about 'life' in the broad, summarizing manner of, say, George Eliot. Indeed, purging her original idea of an omniscient narrator could be read as the ejection of the Victorian influence from the work, of its calm, ordering effect.

Looked at another way, however, the work seems very far from a modernist assertion of artifice. For Woolf would perhaps claim that this presentation of indeterminacy was nothing more than an accurate representation of reality, a super-mimesis. In this she is not so very far away from the post-structuralist speculations of someone like Roland Barthes. The fluid and dissolvent nature of the work, its bewildering multiplicity tend to rob us of the comfortable notions of completion and closure which we normally associate with fictional texts, precisely in order to do justice to Woolf's own sense of the provisionality and uncertainty of 'life itself'. In this view, what *The Waves* offers is a scrupulously honest presentation of the baffling nature of actual experience, albeit in a 'concentrated' form. We are on the way to a proper understanding of the work when we perceive that part of its purpose is to undermine the conventional form of the novel so as to dramatize the process of human life; the 'moments' of ecstatic being are crossed by the muddled and confusing efforts to gain a true sense of direction without ever quite reaching a sense of certainty. In this sense the work is radically mimetic and radically a-fictional, yielding up the artificial satisfactions of coherence and completion for the sake of a higher order of verisimilitude.

And yet – how could it be otherwise – *The Waves* is a work of art, it does have a 'shape' and completion. It is fitting that the closure is given to the waves, as the last line – 'The waves broke on the shore' – completes the pattern, framing the soliloquies entirely within the interludes. This ending, added between the final draft and the published book, has generated much critical commentary about whether Bernard's final splendid speech is wholly undermined or not. Its enigmatic quality is likely to continue to fuel this debate. But what cannot be in doubt is the sense of formal resolution which the ending gives to the work. The book works against any coherent final statement, yet paradoxically is itself a sustained and coherent whole, holding together in a 'globe' of balanced tensions and 'essential' contradiction a harmonious form. Woolf had reason to feel that she had made a cast at her 'vision'. There does emerge from the confusing welter of the waves a sense of the awful brevity of human life, but also a sense of its splendour, and the 'effort' of defiance it achieves. The book offers a vision of 'life itself', a statement, if never a final one, on the 'essence of reality', wherein hope and skepticism are finely balanced. *The Waves* is dissolvent, contradictory, confusing, but also a seamless and endlessly absorbing whole.

It is evident that such a rich and complex work offers a variety of possibilities for critical discussion, some of which I have tried to outline in this guide. One may emphasize one aspect or another, particularly in relation to the work's place in the history of the novel. The destruction of coherent meaning and the way in which the fiction undermines itself might be seen in relation to more recent and radical experiments in this direction; emphasizing this aspect makes *The Waves* seem a progenitor of postmodernism. Yet, as I have tried to show, the work also looks back with something like longing to 'the novel', the ordered shape arising from a more coherent world. What is I think essential in any interpretation of *The Waves* is to perceive the paradoxical union of these two elements, the sense in which the work, with great difficulty, manages to contain both. This makes the work particularly of its time – or perhaps we ought to say, in deference to Virginia Woolf, of its moment. Perhaps this is why the work has had so little influence; the particular conjunction between old and new, Victorian and modern, tradition and experiment which informed *The Waves* has passed away, and fiction today has moved toward more parodic, self-reflexive extremes. There are no imitators of *The Waves*; the work, again like *Finnegans Wake*, is *sui generis*. But the brilliance and audacity with which it takes its stand at the crossroad may well prove its most lasting achievement, and secure its place as a landmark of world literature.

Guide to further reading

Primary material

One happy consequence of Virginia Woolf's popularity over the last decade is that she has become one of the best-edited figures of twentieth-century literature. Her complete letters have been published in six volumes (1975–80), edited by Nigel Nicholson and Joanne Trautmann. Her Diary, which is more significant for students of her fiction, has been issued in five volumes (1977–84), superbly edited by Anne Olivier Bell and Andrew McNeillie. Both series are published by the Hogarth Press.

The Hogarth Press similarly keep all of Woolf's fiction in print, along with many ancillary volumes of criticism and reminiscence. Harcourt Brace Jovanovitch, her American publishers, do likewise, and much of her work is available in numerous paperback editions. Among the most important of these are her autobiographical writings, published under the title *Moments of Being*, ed. J. Schulkind (University of Sussex Press, 1976). Unfortunately, to date there has not been the same kind of textual attention and care devoted to her novels as there has been to her biographical material, and the task of providing a standard, corrected edition remains. Of late there has been a spate of attention to early drafts, among the most important of which is J. W. Graham's collation of *The Waves: Two Holograph Drafts* (Hogarth Press, 1976). The essays have also suffered undue neglect. The standard edition remains the four-volume compilation of *Collected Essays* prepared by Leonard Woolf after his wife's death (Chatto and Windus, 1966), though both the selection and editorial practice leave much to be desired. In this edition the first two volumes deal primarily with Virginia Woolf's literary and critical views, and the student may find much here bearing on her view of the novel.

Biography

Among Woolf's many good fortunes was a sensitive and intelligent nephew, who undertook the task of her biography. Quentin Bell's *Virginia Woolf: A Biography*, two volumes (Hogarth Press, 1972–3), is a superbly written effort which will remain the definitive life for many years. Bell studiously avoided literary criticism in his account of Woolf's life, and this gap has begun to be filled by

Lyndall Gordon's *Virginia Woolf: A Writer's Life* (Oxford University Press, 1984). Additional (sometimes odd and eccentric) information can be gleaned from Leonard Woolf's five-volume *Autobiography*, published 1960–9 by the Hogarth Press, and he wrote specifically about *The Waves* from a biographical perspective in *Radio Times*, 28 June 1957. A revisionist handling of the biographical material may be found in Roger Poole's *The Unknown Virginia Woolf* (Cambridge University Press, 1978).

Criticism

There is now substantial critical literature on Virginia Woolf, though in every case quality lags behind quantity. By far the best places to start the study of Woolf are the books by Hermione Lee (*The Novels of Virginia Woolf*, Methuen, 1977) and Michael Rosenthal (*Virginia Woolf*, Routledge & Kegan Paul, 1979). These both are general, balanced, critically acute and readable, avoding the partisan extremes either for or against which have disfigured the history of criticism on Virginia Woolf. The student will find much stimulating and sensitive comment here to guide an initial approach to this author. Erich Auerbach's *Mimesis* (English trans., Princeton University Press, 1953) contains a splendid chapter on Virginia Woolf which is the beginning of any serious critical inquiry.

Among the better specific studies are James Hafley, *The Glass Roof: Virginia Woolf as Novelist* (University of California Press, 1954), and James Naremore, *The World Without a Self* (Yale University Press, 1973). The latter is particularly acute on *The Waves*. Every serious student of this work will want to come to terms with J. W. Graham's essay, 'Point of View in *The Waves*: Some Services of the Style', reprinted in *Virginia Woolf: A Collection of Criticism*, ed. T. Lewis (McGraw-Hill, 1975). Lyndall Gordon's book cited above also has much of interest to say on *The Waves*. Among collections of essays on Woolf's life and work the most useful are the Twentieth Century Views volume, edited by Claire Sprague (Prentice-Hall, 1971), *Virginia Woolf: Revaluation and Continuity*, ed. Ralph Freedman (University of California Press, 1980), and *Virginia Woolf: A Centenary Perspective*, ed. E. Warner (Macmillan, 1983). Two particular essays not included in any collection which recommend themselves to the student of Virginia Woolf are Elizabeth Hardwick's long and interesting piece 'Virginia Woolf and Bloomsbury', which can be found in her book, *Seduction and Betrayal* (Weidenfeld and Nicolson, 1974); and Stuart Hampshire's essay in *Modern Writers* (Chatto and Windus, 1969).

General studies of Modernism are usually full of reference to Virginia Woolf, along the standard lines of emphasizing her outspoken manifesto, 'Modern Fiction'. Among the more intelligent

and engaging considerations of this subject are the short study by
Peter Faulkner, *Modernism* (Methuen, 1977), and the superior col-
lection of extended essays on various aspects of Modernism edited
by Michael Bell, *The Context of English Literature 1900–30*
(Methuen, 1980). The Pelican Guide to English Literature (Penguin,
rev. edn, 1979), vol. 7, is dated in its views as in its Bibliography,
but the introductory chapters are still useful. Joseph Frank's essay,
'Spatial Form in Modern Literature', originally appeared in *The
Sewanee Review*, Vol. 53, 1945, and was reprinted in *Critiques and
Essays in Criticism*, ed. R. W. Chapman (1949).

   With regard to the novel itself, E. M. Forster's *Aspects of the
Novel* (Penguin, 1962) has proved remarkably durable, and a careful
reading will still yield much that is germane about the form. (The
student of Woolf will want to consider her review of the book,
printed in the second volume of her *Collected Essays*.) *Novelists on
the Novel* by Miriam Allott (Routledge and Kegan Paul, 1959) is a
useful collection of comment by practitioners from three centuries,
helpfully collated with long introductions. Frank Kermode's *The
Sense of an Ending* (Oxford University Press, 1967) is a highly
stimulating meditation on the nature of fiction, taken further in the
recent *Essays on Fiction 1971–82* (Routledge and Kegan Paul, 1983).
The long-standing classic in this field is Wayne C. Booth's *The
Rhetoric of Fiction* (University of Chicago, 1961), which opened the
study of the narrator's relation to the tale. This has been extended
in our day to the thoroughgoing study of narrative, which is perhaps
one of the most significant structuralist contributions to literary
criticism. A useful summary of the development of narratology may
be found in Jonathan Culler, 'Story and Discourse in the Analysis
of narrative', in his book *The Pursuit of Signs* (Routledge & Kegan
Paul, 1981). By far the most interesting and useful study of narrative
discipline is Gerard Genette's *Narrative Discourse* (English trans.,
Cornell University Press, 1980). This book, which is a remarkable
and rigorous study of Proust's narrative, is dense and difficult, but
worth the effort. Virginia Woolf, who learned much from Proust,
stands to gain considerably from an application of this approach.